del
12-8-22

DEMCO

Piracy&Plunder

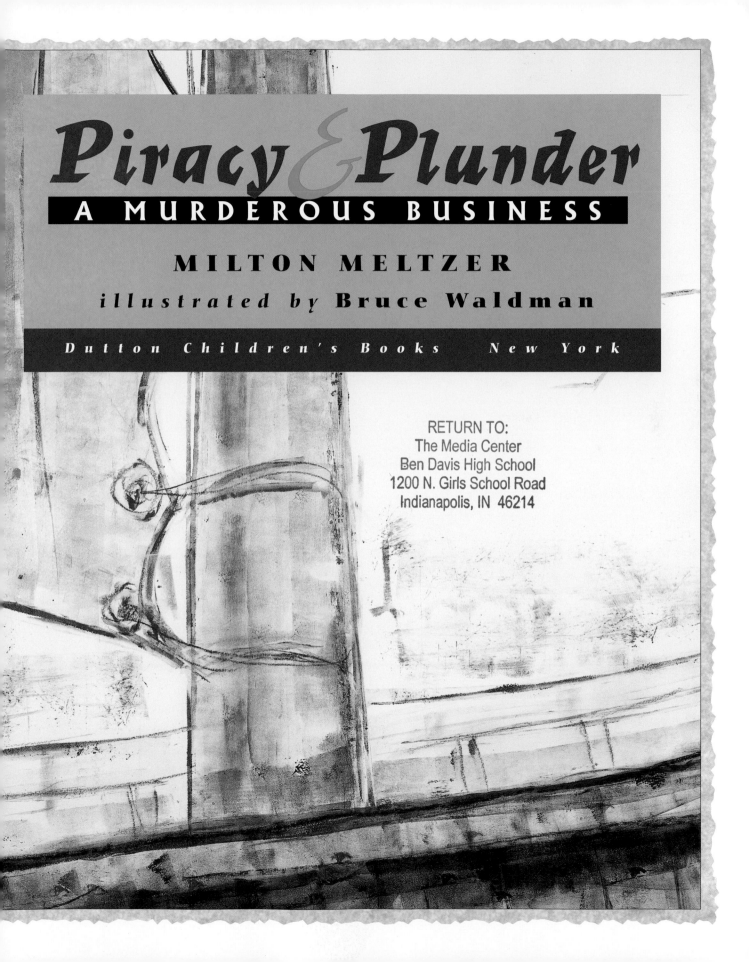

Piracy & Plunder

A MURDEROUS BUSINESS

MILTON MELTZER

illustrated by Bruce Waldman

Dutton Children's Books   New York

Library of Congress Cataloging-in-Publication Data

Meltzer, Milton, date.
Piracy & plunder: a murderous business / Milton Meltzer;
illustrated by Bruce Waldman.
p. cm.
Summary: Surveys the history of pirates, why and how they
became thieves and killers, the lives they led on sea and
on land, the harm they did, and the fates they suffered.
ISBN 0–525–45857–3
1. Pirates—Juvenile literature.
2. Hijacking of ships—Juvenile literature.
3. Pillage—Juvenile literature. [1. Pirates.]
I. Title: Piracy and plunder. II. Waldman, Bruce, ill.
III. Title.   G535.M44 2001
910.4′5—dc21   2001032593

Published in the United States by Dutton Children's Books,
a division of Penguin Putnam Books for Young Readers
345 Hudson Street, New York, New York 10014
www.penguinputnam.com
Designed by Sara Reynolds & Richard Amari
Printed in China. • First Edition
1 2 3 4 5 6 7 8 9 10

CONTENTS

FOREWORD

Many books have been published about pirates. So many that you may wonder, why write still another?

For one good reason. Much of what you may have read about pirates has more to do with romance and fantasy than with reality. Long John Silver, Captain Hook, and their ilk are fun to meet safely in novels or plays, in movies, and on television. But to encounter pirates in real life meant unbearable suffering—beatings, torture, rape, mutilation, execution by strangling or sword or bullet or drowning. Not to mention piracy's main objective—robbery, plunder, loot, ransom, enslavement—whatever could be gained at the victim's cost.

Yet pirates have been so romanticized that a major-league baseball team has no qualms about calling themselves the Pittsburgh Pirates. Those athletes probably don't realize they bear the name of thieves and murderers.

This book aims to tell the true story of pirates and piracy. Readers will find, I think, some unexpected revelations in these pages. Here are the real Blackbeard and Captain Kidd and many other notorious pirates, and here, too, are their crews, women as well as men, who sailed the ships and did the dirty work.

Why and how they became thieves and killers, the lives they led on sea and on land, the harm they did, and the fates they suffered are the stories told here.

Piracy&Plunder

A Plague of Pirates

Piracy is ancient. It is as old as the art of transportation by water. "As in all lands where there are many people, there are some thieves, so in all seas much frequented, there are some pirates." So said Captain John Smith of the Virginia colony, himself once captured by pirates. The same observation was made thousands of years earlier, too. Pirates have cruised the waters and haunted the lives of people at all times and in all parts of the world—in Europe and the Americas, in Asia and Africa, in Australia and the innumerable islands of every sea.

Piracy was, and continues to be, a plague—sometimes devastating and long-lasting, at other times almost gone, only to be revived once again when conditions are ripe.

What is the origin of the word *pirate*? The dictionary says it comes from a Greek word meaning "to attack." Gradually the word came to mean "a person who robs on the sea with violence." Other words—*buccaneer* and *corsair*—came to describe essentially the same kind of seagoing thief.

The Greatest Haul

If anyone could have been called a celebrity back in the 1690s, it was Henry Every. He was the most notorious pirate of his time.

An Englishman, born of poor parents about 1653, Every went to sea as a boy. He learned to read and write, showed a talent for mathematics, and mastered the art of navigation. He served as an officer on merchant ships, including some that engaged in the vile business of the African slave trade.

One day, Every led a mutiny aboard ship. He threw its drunken captain into a small boat, leaving him to find his way to shore. Then he took command of the merchant vessel and launched a career of piracy. The ruthlessness and inhumanity he had seen given free play in the slave trade was apt train-ing for his new business. Every renamed his ship *Fancy* and steered for the Red Sea, where Muslim ships sailed on their way to and from India.

Henry Every

In 1695 Every attacked a huge, heavily armed treasure ship carrying a cargo of gold, silver, jewels, and silks, as well as pilgrims returning home to India after visiting the holy city of Mecca. The *Gang-I-Sawai* was the greatest ship in the Muslim world. She carried 62 guns, 500 soldiers, and 600 passengers. Although outgunned and outnumbered by far, the *Fancy* fired broadsides from its cannon, and a battle began.

The pirates' lucky first shots dis-abled the giant ship, and Every swung his *Fancy* alongside it. His ferocious crew, cutlasses and pistols at the ready, scrambled aboard to fight the waiting Muslim sailors and soldiers. So savage was the pirates' onslaught, and so frightening their reputation, that the Muslims gave in after two hours' resistance. With screams of the wounded and dying rending the air, Every came aboard. He saw blood flow-ing across the decks, and wreckage and the dead lying everywhere. Twenty of his own men were among them.

Not content just to loot the ship, Every let loose an orgy of torture, rape, and murder. His men tore all the clothing off their captives, both men and women. They stole everything their victims had and tortured any they suspected of concealing valuables. In a sadistic rage, the pirates often killed their captives after taking their possessions. They dragged away many of the women and gang-raped them. Savagely abused, some of the women died. Others, shamed by their treatment, stabbed themselves to death or threw themselves into the sea.

When the ravaging was ended, Every had all the Muslims' wealth and the surviving women transferred to the *Fancy*. Sailing southward into safer waters, he and his men divided the loot. Each man in the crew was given a share of what was one of the greatest hauls in the history of piracy.

About a year later, in Ireland, Every deserted his men and disappeared. Some of his crew were later captured and convicted at a trial. Eighteen were sentenced to be transported to Virginia, where they would work as convict labor. Six others were hanged on the gallows.

No one knows where or when or how Henry Every died.

But his name did not die with him. As the sensational news of his deeds circulated in Europe, he became a legend. All sorts of fanciful stories embroidered the truth about him. It was even said that his wealth was so great that he had offered to pay off the national debt of England in exchange for the king's pardoning his crimes. A play about him—*The Successful Pirate*—became a hit. And Daniel Defoe wrote a novel patterned on Every's exploits called *The Life, Adventures and Piracies of the Famous Captain Singleton*.

Homer's Pirate: Odysseus

Was Captain Every's piracy on the Red Sea something new?

Far from it. Pirates on the Red Sea were a problem as far back as 4,000 years ago. That body of water between Africa and the Arabian Peninsula was the spawning ground of a poisonous breed of pirates who sailed in open, undecked ships. The Red Sea was hard to navigate, with few places where a ship in danger could find shelter. It was an important trade route for the

The Battle of Thrace

ancient world. Pirates have continued to prey on commerce in the Red Sea right up to the present.

Egyptian merchant ships sailing down the Red Sea were often the tragic victims of sea rovers. Using hit–and–run tactics, the pirates were even so bold as to swoop down on the shores of the pharaoh's dominion. Sometimes they formed into fleets—like navies—to sack its coastal cities.

In the age that the classical Greek poet Homer wrote about, 4,000 years ago, adventurers made a living at piracy. Piracy became so common that it influenced the development of early Greek civilization. Fearing pirate raids on

the coasts, people moved their settlements inland and built strong walls for protection. A ship owner or merchant would figure in the risk of loss to pirates when making contracts or setting prices.

Literature was soon peppered with tales of piracy. Homer's epic poem *The Odyssey* is an enduring example. When Odysseus lands at Ithaca after 20 years of serving in the Trojan War, he tells of his exploits as a sea raider. Even though he and his men had left Troy with lots of booty, when they came to Thrace they "sacked the city and killed the men and, taking the women and plenty of cattle and goods, divided them up." With nine good ships and crews, he says, he once sailed for five days from Crete to Egypt, where his ships anchored in a river. And then he goes on:

> *I assigned trusty men to guard the ships and sent a scouting party inland...But they, getting too cocky and driven by their greed, immediately began to plunder the smiling countryside, killing men and carrying off women and children. The word soon reached a city: the people heard the shouting and at dawn sailed forth. Soon the whole plain was full of men and horses and the flash of bronze armor....*

These incidents, put in Odysseus' mouth by the poet, were invented, but they told listeners something they knew from their own experience, which happened all too often in the eleventh and twelfth centuries B.C. Not only Egypt, but Cyprus, Phoenicia, Ethiopia, and Libya were among the places where pirate raiders operated. There was so much lawlessness on the seas that trade for a time shrank to almost nothing. Such stories as Homer tells illustrate what sea raiders did in that remote age. Some 2,000 years later, pirates would do the same.

A Thousand Ships

In ancient times one group of pirates became so powerful that they controlled the entire Mediterranean Sea. These were the pirates of Cilicia, a region of southeast Asia Minor that is now the southern part of Turkey. Inland, rugged mountains protected the pirates from attack by land forces. The shoreline offered lofty lookout points to warn of assault from the sea. Around 150 B.C., pirates were operating from Cilicia so successfully that men throughout the region flocked to join the crews and get rich quick.

Centuries before, around 850 B.C., ships superior to those of Homer's time came into use. These were two-banked galleys, with one or two broad square sails. The sails were used mainly for cruising. In battle, with a powerful point-

ed ram jutting from the prow, oarsmen maneu-
vered the ship into position for an attack.

Self-made admirals commanded whole
fleets of pirate ships. They assigned intelligence
agents to ports everywhere, to infiltrate merchant crews and waterfront hangouts. When
the spies found out about shipping plans and
cargoes, they relayed the information back to
pirate headquarters.

But hugely successful raids on shipping
became only a sideline. What profited the
pirates of Cilicia even more was slave-running.
Their ships raided coastal towns mercilessly,
taking hordes of captives and selling them at
the Mediterranean's largest slave market, the
island of Delos. The chief buyers were Roman
plantation owners in need of large stocks of
laborers. So effective were the raids that many
cities paid the pirates protection money to keep
them away.

Meanwhile the regional powers, for one
reason or another, had cut back their navies or
given them up, as Rome had done. So for a time
there was no navy able to wipe out piracy. The pirates commanded over a
thousand ships, all well stocked with weapons and supplies. Spartacus, the
gladiator who led a revolt of 70,000 slaves in 73 B.C., offered bribes to the
Mediterranean pirates to transport part of his forces from the toe of Italy to
Sicily. But they betrayed him, taking his gold and silver and simply sailing off.

Around 70 B.C., the pirates were boldly attacking the shores of Italy, capturing Roman aristocrats. The pirates even smashed their way into Rome's
own port at Ostia, wrecking the warships anchored there and stealing all the

COCKY CAESAR

*One day Cilician pirates seized a ship car-
rying the young Julius Caesar. He was
sailing from Rome to the island of Rhodes to
study law. (His captors could not know that in
the future this aristocrat would become a world-
famous statesman and general and end his days
as dictator of Rome.) The pirates set a high ransom on Caesar. "I'm worth a lot more," he
bragged, so they almost tripled the sum. Send-
ing word to Rome, they kept Caesar on board till
the cash would come. He was so arrogant, so
self-assured, that he ordered the pirates about as
though they were his servants, told them to keep
quiet while he took his naps, practiced his orato-
ry on them, and bawled them out when their
behavior failed to please him.*

*The cocky youngster only amused them,
however, even when he promised laughingly to
return after his release and hang them all.*

*As soon as the ransom money arrived, Caesar
left the ship. Shortly he returned with four ships
and 500 men to scour the sea for his captors.
Those he took prisoner he repaid for their mild
treatment of him by graciously allowing them
to have their throats slit before nailing them to
crosses.*

FOLLOWING PAGE:
Viking ships

pottery, wine, and olive oil the merchants were trying to export. Their raids made the Appian Way, Rome's chief highway, some of which bordered the coast, so unsafe it was rarely used.

By 67 B.C., piracy led to a national crisis in Rome. Desperate, the government gave great powers to the Roman general Pompey, asking him to destroy the pirates in the Mediterranean. He worked out a masterly plan of action, which embraced the vast inland sea. Placing fleets at every sector of the Mediterranean's coastline, he had them attack the pirate strongholds all at once, while his own force of 60 ships swept from Gibraltar eastward, driving the pirates into the jaws of his forces along the shores. Within 40 days the Romans had cleaned up the sea's western end, and Pompey was pursuing the pirates fleeing eastward to their home in Asia Minor. He reached the coast of Cilicia and, laying siege to it, found the exhausted pirates ready to surrender.

Piracy, after centuries of failure to get rid of it, was ended in the Mediterranean for a long time to come.

A Fleet of Ruthless Pagans

"From the fury of the northmen, O Lord, deliver us."

The victims of the Vikings—the piratical Northmen—uttered that heartfelt prayer. From the lands we now know as Norway, Sweden, and Denmark, the Vikings fell upon their victims "with devastation, blood and rapine" for three centuries.

The word *Viking* probably derives from the Norse language; the word came to mean a pirate who lay hidden in fjord, creek, or bay, waiting to pounce upon passing vessels. The rugged mountains and bitter cold of Scandinavia did not make for soft living. Most Northmen were fishermen, farmers, or traders. Some, forced from home by poverty, chose to venture far off in search of necessities plentiful in other places.

From ancient times, bold and hardy men preyed on nearby shipping routes and raided inland villages. When they mastered ship construction and star-

sight navigation they were able to invade waters far from home. The principal object of their raids was plunder—of slaves and silver.

Viking assaults on distant seas began in the year A.D. 793 with a raid upon the small island of Lindisfarne, the most holy place in north England.

A monk named Symeon later wrote an account of the Viking onslaught, based upon oral traditions:

> *A fleet of the pagans arrived in Britain from the north, and rushing hither and thither, and plundering as they went, they slew not only the cattle, but even the priests and deacons, and the choirs of monks and nuns.*
>
> *[On the seventh of the ides of June,] they reached the church of Lindisfarne, and there they miserably ravaged and pillaged everything; they trod the holy things under their polluted feet, they dug down the altars, and plundered all the treasures of the church. Some of the brethren they slew, some they carried off with them in chains, the greater number they stripped naked, insulted, and cast out of doors, and some they drowned in the sea.*

The ships the Vikings learned to build were perfect for their purposes. One of them, unearthed in a tomb in 1903, was very well preserved and is now in a museum in Oslo. Built of oak, it is 71 feet long, 17 feet wide, and 7 feet deep, with 15 pairs of oars, each 12 feet long. Viking sails were large and square. Other Viking ships were probably twice as big—big enough to carry horses, too, so the Northmen could ride far inland in search of loot or places to trade or settle.

Out of Scandinavia came the Viking longships, beaching in Britain, Germany, France, Spain, Iceland, Greenland—and in North America, too, centuries before Columbus sailed west. Vikings crossed the Baltic Sea, south of their own lands, and sailed down the great Russian rivers to reach the land of Byzantium—present-day Istanbul, Turkey.

The men on the rowing benches served as oarsmen at sea and as fighting men on land. Often the Scandinavian shipwrights carved the prows of the long ships into a monstrous dragonhead. Imagine the terror people felt when

Viking pirates   a Viking dragonhead loomed on the horizon, and bearded pirates, notorious for their ruthless ferocity, ran ashore, brandishing their battle-axes.

The degree of hatred for the invaders is seen in this passage from a chronicle written in A.D. 793 at the time Vikings raided Ireland:

> *If a hundred heads of hardened iron could be grown on one neck, and if each head possessed a hundred sharp indestructible tongues of tempered metal, and if each tongue cried out incessantly with a hundred ineradicable loud voices, they would never be able to enumerate the griefs which the people of Ireland—men and women, laymen and priests, young and old—have suffered at the hands of these warlike, ruthless pagans.*

The Vikings who came to Britain initially were summer pirates. They stayed on through the winter because harsh weather at the end of autumn

made the return voyage too risky. Gradually these Viking bands were followed by other Northmen who created permanent settlements. Pirate raids thus shaded into colonizing ventures.

Christian communities suffered most heavily from the Viking raids. The Christians wondered if the atrocities of the heathen men were divine retribution for their sins. The Vikings, however, chose to raid holy places not out of any spiritual opposition but because the treasures of the church and monastery were exposed and undefended.

When the Irish abbot Blathmac heard that the raiders were heading in, he called his monks together to prepare them for martyrdom. The Northmen raged through people's homes, slaughtering everything in their path. Unarmed, Blathmac stood firm when the pirates demanded he tell them where he had hidden the precious metals that enclosed the sacred bones of Saint Columba. He defied them in these words:

I know not of the gold you seek, where it may be placed in the ground, and in what recesses it may be hidden, but, if it were permitted me by Christ to know, never would these lips tell it to your ear. Savagely bring your swords, seize their hilts and kill. O God, I commend my humble self to Thy protection.

Whereupon the savage pirates chopped the abbot to pieces. In 837, Northmen raiding up Irish rivers chose a crossing point on the Liffey as a shore base for their fleets. The earthen ramparts they built to protect their longboats mark the first foundation for the city of Dublin. Similar onshore settlements soon appeared around the coast. These overwintering bases for the pirate bands would one day be known as the Irish cities of Waterford, Wexford, and Limerick. Dublin's rise as the Irish capital was built largely on its importance as a marketplace for the intercontinental Scandinavian slave trade. Amber and furs were brought down from Viking homelands, too, but the chief stock on sale were the slaves captured on Viking raids. Many of these unfortunate people were destined for the Islamic world of the Mediterranean and farther east.

After Alfred the Great, a king of the ninth century, established his supremacy in England, the Vikings turned to the European mainland. They beached first in Belgium, in 878, and then, in the 13 years that followed, according to a chronicle: "There did not exist a road which was not littered with dead, priests and laymen, women, children and babies. Despair spread throughout the land and it seemed all Christian people would perish."

In this period, several Viking chiefs combined their forces into small armies to plunder cities and churches. It was reported in 882 that about 200 Viking ships sailed back home loaded with loot as well as prisoners who could be sold as slaves or ransomed. Viking violence, terrible as it was, was no doubt exaggerated in the telling. But was Viking inhumanity unique? People in that time and in that part of the world—as before then, and in our own time, and almost everywhere in the world—have been capable of appalling cruelties.

Some historians assert that however destructive the Vikings were, as colonists they often made a very positive and significant contribution to the development of western Europe.

Privateers—or Pirates?

The words *pirate* and *privateer* are often tossed around as if they mean the same thing. Well, they do and they don't. You could say that a pirate is not a pirate when he's a privateer. We know what a pirate is. What's a privateer?

A privateer was the name for a privately owned and armed vessel or its commander and crew, cruising under a commission from a government. The commission was called a *letter of marque*. It licensed the privateer to capture or sink merchant vessels of an enemy nation. Privateers in some cases were authorized to keep for their own use whatever they seized from the enemy ships. The justification was that the privateer's sponsor country was only getting even for the harm done to it by an enemy nation.

The custom of licensing private merchant ships to attack and raid enemy merchant ships during wartime seems to have begun back in the thirteenth century. It became more widespread during the reign of England's King Henry

VIII. His daughter, Elizabeth I (1533–1603), continued the practice, for she found it a cheap and easy way to supplement her Royal Navy, which was smaller than England's privately owned merchant fleet.

In that time, merchant ships were built much like warships. They carried cannon, and their crews were trained to fight. Elizabeth could thus expand her sea power while profiting by privateer raids on enemy commerce and coastal cities and towns. By the time Elizabeth came to the throne in 1588, about 400 privateers were operating. During her reign, privateering spread rapidly, with sea captains winning fame and glory for their exploits. Of course the enemy regarded the privateer as a criminal.

Drake: Official Pirate

Privateering was very near piracy. Many privateers were actually merchants trying to make money by capturing enemy ships. Just by holding a letter of marque, the privateer could, under international law, safely commit acts that otherwise would be considered piracy plain and simple.

Maritime powers saw privateering as a cheap way to wage war. Why undertake the vast expense of building and maintaining a large navy if you could rely on merchant captains to attack the enemy?

Besides, privateers often put profits in a sovereign's pocket. A ruler could demand that ship captains hand over some of the ships and goods they seized. Part of the loot was shared with the sovereign, and the rest went to the shipowners, captains, and crews. Privateers were, in effect, a nation's official pirates.

Such a system was bound to be abused. Many a privateer was no more than a licensed pirate. Take Sir Francis Drake. Was he, as the British claimed, the greatest seaman of the Elizabethan age? Or was he also one of its greatest pirates? The very model of the self-made man, Drake would become famous in Europe and America for his privateering. Born in Devonshire in 1540(?), the eldest of 12 sons, Francis was taught to read and write by his father. Early on he showed a deep faith in Protestantism, the official religion of Elizabethan

England. Solidly confident of God's protection, he took risks few others would dare.

In his early teens, Drake was apprenticed to the aging captain of a small coasting vessel carrying freight. He learned much about navigation and how to handle a ship in all kinds of weather. Life at sea was hard, the crew's quarters were tiny and crowded, the food was poor, and sailors were often cold and wet. Drake learned to endure most anything.

Even though of humble birth, a seaman could rise if he was able, conscientious—and lucky. When Drake's captain died, he left his ship to his favorite apprentice. Drake sold it and took work as a purser for his ship–owning kinsman, John Hawkins.

Although late on the scene, Protestant England had begun to contend with Catholic Spain for worldwide empire. With the voyages of Columbus opening the way, Spanish conquistadors had already colonized Central and South America, overcoming the native civilizations and nearly wiping out their people.

Spain's mines in Mexico, Peru, and Bolivia produced fabulous wealth, carried to Spain by annual treasure fleets. Because the mines and plantations of the New World required a very large labor force, unfortunate blacks bought in Africa were shipped across the Atlantic by slave traders of several nations. Slave trading was an immensely profitable business.

Drake's relative, John Hawkins, commanded the first English slaving expeditions to Africa in 1562–65. Sailing to the Spanish colonies in the West Indies, he sold his black cargoes in exchange for hides and silver. It was a brutal, inhuman trade, but that did not trouble Hawkins or his backers. The backers included wealthy merchants, aristocrats, and government officials. And don't forget Queen Elizabeth herself, who gave Hawkins the use of one of her warships, *Jesus of Lubeck*, for the slave trade.

The Spanish claimed an exclusive right to trade in their own colonies in the New World and resented it when Hawkins sailed into the Caribbean without permission. But Hawkins ignored Spanish protests and either paid off or forced colonial officials to do business with him.

The fearless young Drake was delighted when cousin Hawkins signed him

OPPOSITE:

Sir Francis Drake

on for a voyage to Africa and the Caribbean. They seized Portuguese ships they met at sea, killing sailors who resisted them, and looting the cargoes of sugar, ivory, and slaves.

On Hawkins's next venture, he made Drake a principal officer of the Queen's ship the *Jesus*. Hawkins assured Elizabeth he wouldn't attack any foreign ships, but that was only to enable the Queen to deny that she had quietly approved whatever he might do.

While at sea, every morning and every evening Hawkins would gather his crew around the mainmast for religious services. Pious and righteous, all the while he was plundering foreign ships for their slave cargoes and raiding African villages to capture still more slaves. Like most Europeans of their day, the English looked upon the Africans as less than human, as beings who could not experience pain and loss and suffering. Business was business, and this was just another means of making profits.

After a couple of expeditions to the West Indies that brought him little profit, in 1570 Drake tried still another voyage across the Atlantic. This time he sailed with but one ship and a small crew. Now he made his first great haul and returned home a rather rich man. His success led so many others to imitate him that Drake could claim he had launched the great age of British piracy in the Caribbean.

His greatest exploits were yet to come. In 1572, with two small ships and 73 men, he sailed to the isthmus of Panama. Spanish treasure galleons were anchored in the port, ready to be loaded up with gold and silver brought by ship and mule train from Peru and Bolivia. Although suffering several costly mishaps in the swamps and jungle, Drake refused to give up the quest for Spanish treasure.

And then his luck turned. With the aid of escaped black slaves who hated their Spanish masters, his men ambushed three caravans of 190 mules, each mule carrying 300 pounds of silver. He evaded capture by Spanish ships cruising off the coast and returned to England with the immense plunder.

Famous and wealthy as he had become, Drake had no feeling that enough is enough. In 1577, he set out with five ships to raid Spanish settlements on the Pacific coast. He sailed across the Atlantic and down the coast of South America, where he lost two ships but managed to navigate the Strait of Magellan (at the southern end of South America)—the first Englishman to do so. Another ship and its crew were lost, and then a fourth became separated from Drake and called it quits, sailing for home. Going on alone in his flagship, the *Golden Hind*, Drake plundered Spanish settlements and ships on the west coast of North America wherever he found them. Then he made a great leap into the unknown and decided to cross the Pacific and reach home by sailing all the way around the world. (His would be only the second ship in history to accomplish that. Magellan's was the first.) He rounded Africa's Cape of Good Hope and, at last, after nearly three years away, reached England on September 26, 1580.

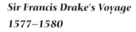

Sir Francis Drake's Voyage
1577–1580

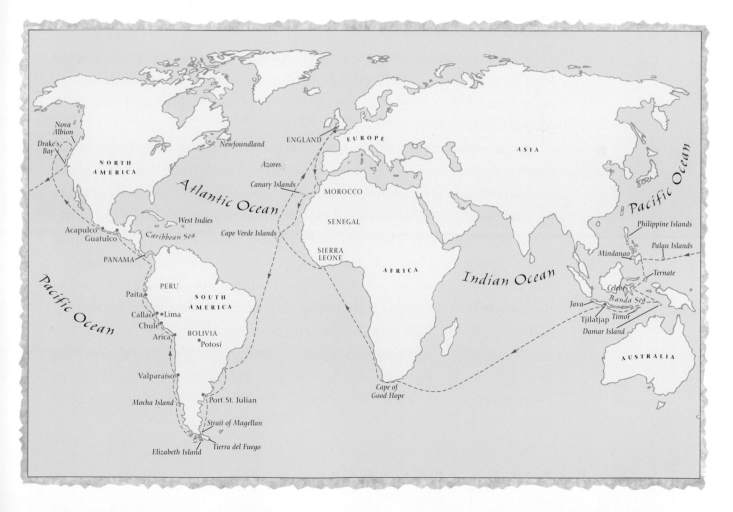

And once more, with fabulous treasure aboard. The Queen and the other backers of the voyage received a handsome return on their investment in what amounted to piracy. Drake and the crew took their share of loot, of course. The excitement created by the reports of his adventure made him a hero, the favorite of the Queen, and an authority on maritime matters. Elizabeth honored him with knighthood.

This national adulation made Drake, who had always been a vain man, an even bigger braggart. Still, he would have more to boast about. In 1588, when the Spanish Armada sailed against England, the two veteran pirates Admiral Sir John Hawkins and Vice Admiral Sir Francis Drake of the British fleet would play major roles in defeating the invaders.

A Cozy Connection

The cozy connection between Queen Elizabeth and Francis Drake—both profiting from piracy—found its echo in the British colonies of America. Here, too, government officials and enterprising businessmen gave silent, and sometimes even public, blessings to piracy.

England's attempt to clamp tight government controls on her colonies in North America encouraged piracy. From 1647 on, the various English Navigation Acts tried to prevent the colonists from manufacturing "so much as a nail for a horseshoe." The laws ordered that all goods be imported from the mother country. England's industries and merchants wanted to sell at the highest prices possible and buy colonial raw materials at the lowest prices possible. This attempt at monopoly roused colonial resistance. Smuggling began, and so did trading with privateers and pirates, who brought into port the goods they had looted on the high seas. The Crown's port officials and even local governors conspired to participate in the illegal trade. New York's royal governor, Benjamin Fletcher, handed out commissions to privateers and took his slice of their profits. Pirates sailed as far off as the Red Sea to steal goods and bring

them home, handing a share to local officials in the ports. The corrupt Governor Fletcher was so bold as to entertain in his home the notorious pirate Thomas Tew. When London reproved him, the governor replied that he was only trying to cure Captain Tew of his drinking and his "vile habit of swearing."

Soon piracy in colonial America infested the shores, bays, and islands of the Atlantic coast from Newfoundland in the north to Key West in the south. The geographical nature of the coastline helped make piracy "a natural American sport." And so did the irresistible desire for quick riches. The predatory business that began in the 1600s was what would later be called a *racket*—that is, an alliance between violators of the law and the agents of government. Merchants and pirates joined together in buying the government, whether of New York, Boston, Newport, or any other port. It became customary for pirates to hand rich gifts to governors in return for protection. Governor Fletcher, for example, accepted silver and jewels from the pirate Robert Coats.

Blackbeard

Leading citizens of the Carolinas were just as friendly to pirates as Governor Fletcher of New York had been. Take their connection with Edward Teach, alias "Blackbeard," one of the wildest villains in the pirate business. So many weird tales are told about him that it is hard to sift out the facts.

Teach was known as Blackbeard because his jet-black beard completely covered his face, even going around his eyes. He made the most of the fierce look, twisting the ends of his hair into small pigtails and turning them around his ears. He would place hemp cord under his pirate hat, then set the ends on fire when he confronted victims, glaring at them so madly that they would believe he was the very devil himself.

Born in England, Edward Teach went to sea as a youngster. Around 1716, he served on a pirate ship that captured several vessels between the West Indies and the American mainland. With his pirate chief's approval, he took

Blackbeard command of a captured ship and began his independent piratical career. His reputation as one of the boldest pirates soared when he defeated a British warship in a bloody battle lasting several hours.

Building up a squadron of four or five ships, Blackbeard worked along the coast of the Carolinas. Once, within a few days, he captured five ships off Charleston, terrifying the city's inhabitants. The merchant ships in the harbor were so scared of the notorious Blackbeard that they refused to leave anchor–age, and all commerce was suspended.

Blackbeard then moved up the coast of North Carolina, hiding in and operating from its many coves. It was suspected that he avoided capture by paying off various officials.

In an effort to cut down on piracy, King George of England proclaimed that pirates who promised to quit their "profession" could obtain a certificate exempting them from punishment for past deeds. Blackbeard hastened to take advantage of the offer, but with no intention of keeping his promise. Governor Charles Eden of the Carolinas had his court declare Blackbeard an honest privateer, a farcical decision that more than hinted at corruption.

Very few pirate captains had wives or families, but Blackbeard, reputed to have been married 13 times, took a fancy to a girl of 16, and Governor Eden readily performed the marriage ceremony. At the wedding party, the pirate crew shocked the girl's family by carousing, gambling, and drinking for several days running.

Sobering up, with winter coming on, Blackbeard headed his fleet toward the milder West Indies. They captured five ships, English and French, sailed back to the Carolinas, and shared the loot with Governor Eden.

One incident illustrates Blackbeard's insane behavior. Drinking in the ship's cabin with a friend one evening, he suddenly pulled out a pistol. Holding it under the table, Blackbeard shot the man in the knee, crippling him for life. "Why did you injure your friend?" he was asked by a crew member. "If I do not now and then kill one of you," Blackbeard is said to have replied, "you'll forget who I am."

Planters and merchants who had suffered great losses from Blackbeard's raids finally got fed up. Knowing how corrupt the Carolinas governor was, they appealed to Governor Alexander Spotswood of Virginia for help. He sent out two armed sloops, crewed by 61 men of the British navy, to capture the pirates.

The two forces met at Ocracoke Inlet, off the coast of North Carolina, in November 1718. A broadside from Blackbeard's flagship, which had 40 guns, disabled one sloop, killing or wounding 16 of the British sailors. When the cannon smoke cleared, Blackbeard moved his ship alongside the other sloop and, with 14 of his men, jumped aboard. A bloody hand-to-hand struggle began, with sabers flashing and pistol shots exploding. Nearly every man was bathed in blood when the sloop's officer, Lt. Robert Maynard, came to grips with Blackbeard. The pirate chief kept firing his three pistols as sabers slashed him. Even with 20 saber cuts and five shots in him, Blackbeard continued fighting, until one of Maynard's men, with a great swoop of his broadsword, cut off his head. When they saw they had lost their leader, the surviving pirates surrendered or jumped into the sea.

On Lt. Maynard's order, the pirate's bearded head was suspended below the sloop's bowsprit. When that grisly trophy came into view at the harbor, the crowd roared its gratitude. But did Blackbeard's death mean that the colonists were free of piracy? Hardly. There was no exact count, of course, but between 1,500 and 2,000 pirates were operating at that time in North America and Caribbean waters.

Blackbeard's loot was recovered from his ships, and the small fortune shared among victorious sailors. Fourteen of his pirates were hanged at the waterfront. In his two years as a pirate, Blackbeard had plundered about 20 ships, but never made a grand haul, such as Henry Every's. Yet his weird looks and behavior made him the most famous of all pirates.

Speed, Surprise, Terror

What kinds of ships did pirates use? It depended on many things.

Basically, a ship is a platform that will stay afloat. Throughout history, inventive minds have designed a variety of ships, reflecting the technology and materials available, the uses to which the ships will be put, and the nature of the weather and water in the operating zones.

Wind offers free power. The earliest pirates used ships with sails. But pirates needed to get close enough to their prey for hand-to-hand fighting. And for that, ships propelled by oars were much better. Then, too, a pirate chief needed a ship big enough to store supplies of food and water for his crew.

We've seen which ships pirates used in the ancient world, and later how the Vikings designed longships for their distant sea raids. As time passed, pirates used whatever ships they could steal. What they wanted most were

ships that were fast, well armed, and seaworthy under any and all conditions. Ships that could make ocean crossings were highly desirable.

To catch their prey and then make a quick getaway, pirates found sloops useful. These were long, slender boats with a single mast, usually so fast they could outsail any pursuer. In the Mediterranean, galleys once were common. Low, seagoing vessels, they were powered by oars. Slaves captured by the pirates usually did the rowing.

When merchant sailing ships were unable to move for lack of wind, they were easy prey for pirate galleys, whose oar power made them very maneuverable. When the wind rose, pirates could hoist a large sail on the single mast of their galley. Guns mounted in the bows and along the rails provided firepower. Many galleys were big enough to carry a hundred fighting men.

Along the North American coast, pirates favored the schooner. These vessels were rigged fore and aft, at first only with two masts, later with three or more, and with square topsails. In the 1600s, the British and Dutch created the model schooner, but in a few decades the colonists in America developed a speedier type. More maneuverable, they were still big enough to carry many guns and a large crew.

Usually, the bigger the ship, the better pirates liked it. Large ships could carry more guns, move faster, and ride out storms. Yet smaller craft had their advantages, too. They were easier to beach and to "heel over" for cleaning and repairs. Small ships could be hidden in creeks or estuaries where pursuing warships could not navigate.

Pirates could not walk into a shipyard and order the vessel they wanted. So their fleets were stolen—"prizes," pirates called them—and adapted, if necessary, to the needs of piracy. Often, after looting a ship, if the pirates had no use for it, they set it adrift or burned it.

In the West Indies, pirates preferred to attack in open boats. They adapted these from canoes the local fishermen used. They were really dugouts carved from tree trunks. The bigger canoes, which could carry up to 25 men, were either rowed or operated with a single sail. In the late 1600s, pirates used canoes to attack Spanish coastal settlements. Lookouts on shore had difficulty

spotting these low, narrow vessels coming in over the horizon. It's hard to think of canoes as fighting ships, but in one case pirates were able to defeat three Spanish warships by massing their canoes, sweeping close to the big ships, and firing their long-barreled muskets with such accuracy that they devastated the Spanish crews.

But good ships are useless without good men. Where did the pirate chiefs get their crews? And what kind of men were they?

Who Pirates Were

Romantic tales usually portray pirates as soldiers of fortune or wronged noblemen seeking justice. Or as anything but what they really were (and are).

The truth is, most pirates were plain men who had gone to sea as boys. Even the most famous pirate chiefs began their careers as ordinary seamen. Only after they turned to piracy was their talent for command discovered by the men who elected them to leadership. For in such a society of outlaws, merit, not birth, counted most.

But why become a pirate?

Some sailors came to it after deserting the navy. Often they had been "press-ganged" in the first place; that is, forced to join the navy against their wishes. Or perhaps they deserted because they couldn't tolerate the harsh discipline aboard a warship. Then there were the seamen serving on a merchant ship captured by pirates. If these men looked strong and bold, they were invited to join the pirate crew.

Mutiny was another path to piracy. Merchant seamen who dared to mutiny would seize the ship of their captain, get rid of him, and sail off under the pirate flag. They were the toughest of all pirates, for when they mutinied, they knew hanging would be the punishment if they were caught. Yet men took that great risk because they knew society did not respect the labor of ordinary seamen. They had no hope of ever rising above that lowest of posi-

OPPOSITE:

A pirate schooner

tions. In the huge merchant fleets of colonial empires, seamen sweated out a life so cruel that they often came to hate the shipowners and ship captains.

Children, too, often served on pirate ships. When the sea raiders plundered coastal villages, they might capture boys as young as ten or twelve to serve the officers as cabin boys or to be apprenticed to craftsmen, such as the ships' carpenters. Mostly, though, it was teenagers pirates forced into service. In battle, the teenagers had an important job to do: they fed the powder and shot to the gunners. When booty was distributed among the crew, the youngest, too, got their share. In the seventeenth and eighteenth centuries in England, children of the poorer classes commonly worked as servants, apprentices, or farm laborers. If dissatisfied with their lot, they fled from their masters and wandered the roads, towns, and cities. Inevitably some turned to piracy as a life with richer promise.

That was the main reason most men turned to piracy—the chance of getting rich through plunder. Isn't that what draws all thieves into their trade? But there was another reason, too: the desire for revenge upon the cruel and unjust society most pirates had suffered under. You could see that in the very names pirates chose for their ships: *Revenge, Holy Vengeance, Defiance, Black Revenge.*

Merchants and planters in the colonies of Virginia and the West Indies were always short of labor and were eager to take anybody offered to them. Kidnappers in English cities would snatch children off the streets and ship them to new masters abroad for a good price. If pirates captured the transport, the unwilling emigrants were often not reluctant to join up with these lawbreakers.

Going to sea was never an easy calling, certainly in the days before seamen's unions and government regulations improved conditions aboard ships. The crews lived scarcely better than slaves. Small pay, scanty, awful food and water, and brutal discipline made many an honest sailor ready to turn pirate. Mary Read, a female pirate (we'll hear more of her later) was asked by her captain (before he knew she was a women) why she followed a life so full of danger and the near certainty that one day she would be hanged. What she answered was reported thus:

As to the hanging she thought it no great hardship, for were it not for that, every
cowardly fellow would turn pirate and so infest the seas that men of courage would
starve. That if it was put to her choice, she would not have the punishment less
than death, the fear of which kept dastardly rogues honest; that many of those who
were now cheating the widows and orphans and oppressing their poor neighbors
who had no money to obtain justice, would then rob at sea and the ocean would be
as crowded with rogues as the land, so that no merchant would venture out, and
the trade in the little time would not be worth following.

Unemployment was another reason seamen turned to piracy. When James
I became King of England in 1603, after the death of Elizabeth, he decided
peace was better than war. Then why spend money on building up the navy?
He also stopped the practice of privateering. Soon after, he banned all English
seamen from seeking work on foreign ships. Rather than starve, jobless sea–
men became pirates. No wonder men became outlaws, wrote Captain John
Smith in 1630:

Some, because they became slighted of those for whom they had got much wealth;
some for that they could not get their due; some, for that had lived bravely, would
not abase themselves to poverty; some vainly, only to get a name; others for
revenge, covetousness, or as ill; and as they found themselves more and more
oppressed, their passions increasing with discontent, made themselves turn pirate.

By 1618, there were ten times as many English pirates as there had been
during the whole long reign of Queen Elizabeth.

Captain Smith understood what drove most men to lawlessness when he
urged all merchants and their men not to be sparing of decent pay for their
men, "for neither soldiers nor seamen can live without means, but necessity
will drive them to steal, and when they are once entered into that trade, they
are hardly reclaimed." It was but one small step from poverty to piracy.

And finally, Bartholomew Roberts echoed what others said when he told
why men in his time turned to piracy. "In an honest service there is thin

FOLLOWING PAGES:
Children serving on
a pirate ship

rations, low wages, and hard labor; in this [piracy], plenty, satiety, pleasure and ease, liberty and power; and who would not balance creditor on this side, when all the hazard that is run for it, at worst, is only a sour look or two at choking? No, a merry life and a short one shall be my motto."

Life Aboard Ship

What was life like if you joined a pirate crew?

Many of the men who came aboard expected a freer life than they had known on merchant ships or in the navy. But in certain respects, life aboard pirate ships was as hard as on any other ship in the age of sail.

Belowdecks it was always dark, the only light coming from flickering candles. The holds stank of bilgewater and rotting meat. In rough weather the sea poured down the hatchways. As many as 200 men might be wedged into small quarters. The sweat and dirt of unwashed bodies created nauseating odors.

Many ships had no kitchen, so food was cooked in a cauldron, dangerous to use when weather was rough. Without refrigeration there was no way to preserve fresh food. And the food itself? Biscuits usually rotten with mold. Beef swarming with worms and maggots, washed down with beer or wine. If there was fresh meat, it was usually turtle or tuna caught in the Caribbean. Some ships might carry hens, to provide fresh eggs and meat. But sometimes pirate ships ran out of supplies, and weeks or months would pass before the pirates could seize a ship and provision themselves. There is a report of starving pirates who roasted scraps of leather and gobbled down the unchewable bits. At times, driven to desperation by hunger, pirates risked attacking far bigger ships, carrying many more men and guns.

Rats, roaches, and other vermin made disease a daily danger. Typhus, malaria, and dysentery were common hazards, too. (And there were no medicines to cure them.) Scurvy, caused by a lack of vitamin C found in fresh fruit and vegetables, was another menace.

At sea, you had to endure endless hours, days, weeks, even months of boredom in between those wildly exciting times when you seized a prize. Before and after, your eyes saw only monotonous stretches of empty sea and sky. All the while you were penned in with the same faces, the same talk—or worse, the same silence. Out of boredom and frustration bloody quarrels often erupted. Drunkenness was commonly a great relief from the boredom. Pirates drank as much and as often as they liked, whether on sea or land. They prized the freedom to drink as their personal right. So alcoholism was rampant, and many died of it.

Pirates drinking

Pirates drank huge quantities of brandy, rum, gin, wine, and beer. A stiff dose of alcohol helped a man forget that any day his life might end on the gallows. One irate captain in a drunken frenzy ashore began chopping off the arms and legs of bystanders. Another drunken captain sliced the ears off a merchant ship's captain, and after salting and peppering them, made his victims eat them. Note, however, that drunkenness for centuries was just as common in civilian life as on pirate ships.

While brawling might break the monotony, worse things could happen. You could fall from the rigging and be crippled or killed. A storm could wash you overboard. Your ship could crash on the rocks or collide with a glacier. And fire—aboard wooden ships, this was always a possibility.

Yet there was still another danger. Your business was to pillage and loot. But not every victim gave up without a fight. Nor was any pirate safe from capture. Take Captain Thomas Pound, a pirate who robbed vessels off the coast of New England. In 1689, during a fight with a sloop sent out to end Pound's raids, the pirate ship was captured, with this damage to the crew reported:

Pound—shot in the side and arm

Johnston—shot in the jaw

Buck—seven holes shot through his arms

Siccadam—shot through both legs

Griffin—shot in the ear, the bullet coming out through his eye, which he lost

Lander—shot through an arm

Warren—shot in the head

Dipper—killed

Darby—killed

Hill—killed

Watkins—killed

Lord—killed

Daniels—killed

Phips—wounded in the head

Brown—wounded in the hand

Only one of the pirates was convicted on trial and executed. Another was found not guilty, and the rest were declared guilty but pardoned on payment of a fee.

As for Captain Pound himself, he was found guilty but reprieved, and then sent to England, where the charge against him was dismissed. He was given command of a ship. A few years later, he died, "honored and respected."

A Democracy of Thieves

Any group of people engaged in a common effort develops some sort of structure or organization. Pirates—thieves, cutthroats, brutes though they were— had a strange kind of brotherhood. They hated the laws and the discipline of the oppressive world they had escaped from. So in their pirate realm, they insisted on a democracy, where every man's individual rights were respected.

Didn't they all have to work together to capture their prize? Then, of course, they all would have an equal voice in making decisions. Whether to fight or to flee, whether to anchor here or there, whether to cruise in the Caribbean or in the Red Sea—all such decisions were voted upon.

Even the choice of captain was the product of a democratic process. A pirate crew elected all their ship's officers, and by their vote could remove them from office whenever they chose. Ship's officers could wear no special uniform nor use any other marks of distinction. The captain had his own cabin, but any of the crew was free to enter it at any time.

As the novelist Daniel Defoe wrote: "They only permit him to be captain, on condition that they may be captain over him." It's known that on one pirate voyage, the captain was changed a dozen times.

There were other important posts aboard ship. The quartermaster had almost equal responsibility with the captain. Usually an experienced seaman and expert navigator, he handled the helm when the ship was sailing. He supervised the disposition of plunder—what to take from the captured ship, what to keep, and what to sell. And he saw to it that every crew member got his fair share.

Captain and quartermaster had the authority to appoint men with special skills: the sailing master, the boatswain, the gunner, the carpenter, the sail-maker, the surgeon. (Surgery amounted to cutting off injured arms or legs, a duty the carpenter often carried out.) Most popular among the crew were musicians, who could accompany song and dance with fiddle, pipe, or horn.

Pirates were mostly young men. In the early 1700s, their average age was twenty-seven. That was also the average age of the men in the merchant marine and the Royal Navy. You had to have the strength and agility of youth to meet the hardships of life at sea in all kinds of weather.

Pirate musicians

Pirate crews were commonly multinational. In the crew of the famous pirate captain Henry Morgan, there were Dutch, French, Italian, Portuguese, and British seamen. Several of his men were blacks. Blacks were well represented on many pirate ships. Some were equal partners in their crew; others were slaves, taken from captured slave ships or on raids of coastal settlements, and used as servants, often given the hardest and most menial work to do.

Physical toughness and courage in combat were demanded of all, from cabin boy to captain. No one was excused from battle. Signs of weakness or fear of fighting brought ridicule, abuse, or worse. No matter what the size of the crew—whether ten men or 200 men—quarters were so confined that everyone knew all about everyone else.

A Code of Conduct

A code of conduct? On pirate ships?

Yes. Though they freely violated society's laws, pirates created a well-regulated system of rules to govern their relations with one another. All pirate ships operated under "codes of conduct" that spelled out the rights and duties of the crew, from captain to cabin boy. From ship to ship, the codes were much the same. Just like the citizens of any community, pirates knew what was expected of them and what was not acceptable, no matter what ship they sailed on or what port they anchored in.

Bartholomew Roberts, a pirate captain of the early eighteenth century, worked out this covenant, which all his crew had to swear to abide by:

> *I. Every man shall have an equal vote in affairs of moment. He shall*
> *have an equal title to the fresh provisions of strong liquors at any*
> *time seized, and shall use them at pleasure unless a scarcity may make*
> *it necessary for the common good that a retrenchment may be voted.*
> *II. Every man shall be called fairly in turn by the list on board of*
> *prizes, because over and above their proper share, they are allowed a*

shift of clothes. But if they defraud the company to the value of even one dollar in plate, jewels or money, they shall be marooned. If any man rob another he shall have his nose and ears slit, and be put ashore where he shall be sure to encounter hardships.

III. None shall game for money either with dice or cards.

IV. The lights and candles should be put out at eight at night, and if any of the crew desire to drink after that hour they shall sit upon the open deck without lights.

V. Each man shall keep his piece, cutlass and pistols at all times clean and ready for action.

VI. No boy or woman to be allowed amongst them. If any man shall be found seducing any of the latter sex and carrying her to sea in disguise he shall suffer death.

VII. He that shall desert the ship or his quarters in time of battle shall be punished by death or marooning.

VIII. None shall strike another on board the ship, but every man's quarrel shall be ended on shore by sword or pistol in this manner. At the word of command from the quartermaster, each man being previously placed back to back, shall turn and fire immediately. If any man does not, the quartermaster shall knock the piece out of his hand. If both miss their aim they shall take to their cutlasses, and he that draweth first blood shall be declared the victor.

IX. No man shall talk of breaking up their way of living till each has a share of £1,000. Every man who shall become a cripple or lose a limb in the service shall have 800 pieces of eight from the common stock and for lesser hurts proportionately.

X. The captain and the quartermaster shall each receive two shares of a prize, the master gunner and boatswain, one and one-half shares, all other officers one and one-quarter, and private-gentlemen of fortune one share each.

XI. The musicians shall have rest on the Sabbath Day only by right. On all other days by favour only.

A duel

Tactic of Terror

Pirates hunting for their prey relied on surprise, speed, and terror for success. They preferred to use ships built for speed, such as schooners and sloops. But they knew how to modify other kinds to attain velocity and maneuverability. Swift ships, heavily armed, could almost always overcome the slower cargo vessels they stalked.

Pirates used deception to catch victims unaware. A common trick was to fly the flag of a friendly nation, then hoist the pirate's black flag only at the last moment. Or, keeping their guns hidden, they would pose as slow-moving merchant or passenger ships as they came within sight of a prize.

When their lookout spotted a victim, pirates did not attack at once. They watched the ship closely for hours or even days: How fast could it sail? What armament did it have? What kind of cargo might it be carrying? Was resistance likely?

If the pirates decided to attack, they moved swiftly to overtake the prize; coming in close, they fired a warning shot and demanded surrender. When, as happened rarely, a prize refused to give in, the pirates fired on it—at first, only to disable masts and rigging. Why sink the cargo they wanted to capture? If they were defied, they fired a broadside from their heavy guns as well as a volley of small shot. Bombardment usually did such great damage to the hull, rigging, and sails, as well as the crew on deck, that the prize surrendered.

The reputation for brutality and terror that clung to pirates gave them a special advantage in their encounters with merchant ships. Few seamen wanted to fight to save the cargo of a rich man's ship. They knew that to resist a pirate attack was to invite torture and death. Better to surrender and go on living.

The reverse was true for pirates. They fought savagely when resisted, knowing that their lives and their enrichment depended on victory.

When a pirate ship fell short of skilled men, it often forced craftsmen it found on a captured ship to join its crew. Rarely did such men go willingly. One news report of 1725 tells of a sloop sailing from Boston to the West Indies that was captured by pirates. Boarding the sloop, the pirates "invited" Ebenezer Mower, a craftsman, to join them. To make sure he'd come, they beat him over the head with the blunt side of an ax and, as he lay bruised and bloodied on the deck, held the ax over him, threatening to chop his head off if he did not sign the ship's articles. He signed....

There are countless examples of such terrifying tactics. (Remember what the pirate captain Henry Every allowed his men to do to the passengers and crew of the *Gang-I-Sawai*.) Some pirates set fire to their victims. Shot them out of a cannon. Cut off their ears, nose, or limbs. Blinded them. Used a sailing needle to sew up a man's lips. Forced captives to run round and round the

ship's mast till they died of exhaustion. Made a merchant captain drink bottle after bottle of rum till he staggered overboard and drowned. Cut open a victim's stomach, tied one end of his intestines to a post, and, beating him with a burning stick, made him dance till it pulled out the rest of his guts.

And what about the punishment of marooning?

Marooning

Every pirate code of conduct called for "marooning" anyone in the crew who deserted the ship in time of battle or otherwise acted treacherously. The guilty person was set onshore in some uninhabited, isolated place, often a desert island. Perhaps he was allowed to have a gun, a few bullets, and a flask of water—but nothing else except the clothes he wore.

If left on a sandy bit of land, the marooned pirate would likely die of agonizing thirst and dehydration, or starvation. If he was marooned along a shipping lane, there was the chance of being picked up someday.

What often comes to mind when we think of lonely existence on a desert island is *Robinson Crusoe*, Daniel Defoe's enduringly popular story, published in 1719. Yet the fictional Crusoe is not a pirate. He is cast ashore when his ship is wrecked, and all on board perish but himself. Defoe's hero lives for 28 years on a desert island off the coast of South America. It is a fascinating story of man's ability to survive, constructed with such masterful attention to detail that it seems utterly true.

There is, however, a connection between Crusoe and a real pirate, Alexander Selkirk (1676–1721). This Scottish seaman served on a pirate ship, quarreled violently with its captain, and when they dropped anchor off an island in the South Pacific west of Chile, he demanded to be set ashore because he thought the ship unseaworthy. Luckily, Selkirk found himself on an island with a good supply of water and many wild pigs and goats. Still, he was all alone for five

years, until a privateer commanded by Captain Woodes Rogers found him, clothed in sheepskins, looking like a wild man.

Rogers added Selkirk to his crew and continued capturing prizes. Finally, three years later, Selkirk landed in London. Captain Rogers made Selkirk's story part of his own book, *A Cruising Voyage Around the World*, published in 1712. It was full of the details of the man's ingenious struggle to survive in so desolate a place.

It seems certain that Defoe had read that book when he set out to create his own version of how a shipwrecked man learns to overcome the terrible mental and physical challenges of isolation. To make Crusoe's survival more credible, Defoe gives him a companion, Friday. Defoe's book was instantly popular, and it has continued to enthrall readers for nearly 300 years.

The Honorable Sir Henry Morgan

He died peacefully in bed in 1628, at home on the huge estate he owned on the island of Jamaica. When his funeral procession reached the cemetery, and his coffin was interred, a 22-gun salute was fired by a ship of the Royal Navy, followed by another salute from all the merchant ships in the harbor.

Thus was Sir Henry Morgan honored. Despite a notorious career as the most famous buccaneer of his time, he had been knighted by Charles II, King of England, and served the Crown as deputy governor of Jamaica.

Call him buccaneer or call him pirate. It came to the same thing. The buccaneers were a diverse lot of men—runaway slaves, a few Indians who had escaped extermination, ex-convicts, deserters—who lived as nomads, hunting the wild pigs and cattle on the island of Hispaniola. They traded meat and hides with passing ships for powder, shot, guns, and knives. Their name comes from the Arawak word *boucan* for the wooden grill used to dry meat by smoking. Hence *boucanier* or buccaneer.

When the Spanish who ruled the island tried to drive them out, the buccaneers formed gangs and turned to the sea for a pirate's livelihood. Operating from various bases in the Caribbean, they attacked and looted Spanish ships and colonies.

Respecting no laws but their own, the buccaneers soon drew more men much like themselves—castaways, victims of shipwrecks, deserters, servants fleeing their masters, and fugitive slaves—to their "Brotherhood of the Coast." Life was cheap in that region, but the buccaneers took the prize for cruelty. One of their chiefs, François L'Olonnois, so terrified the Spanish that they chose to die rather than surrender to him. He enjoyed torturing captives by gradually cutting them to pieces. Once he cut open the breast of a Spanish prisoner, pulled out his heart with his hands, and gnawed it with his teeth, like a wolf. Another buccaneer roasted two Spanish farmers over a spit when they refused to show him where they kept their pigs.

Sir Henry Morgan

Was Henry Morgan like that?

He was born into a farm family in Wales about 1635. In his youth he joined the British army, serving in a failed attempt to capture Hispaniola from the Spanish. The expedition then moved off to attack poorly defended Jamaica and took it easily. Both the Royal Navy and privateers used the new British colony as a base for their operations.

Commissioned by Jamaica's governor as a privateer, Morgan was licensed to attack Spanish ships but not Spanish towns. Still, his savage raids on Spanish towns in Central America proved so profitable that the British authorities pretended not to know about them.

At the age of thirty-two, on account of his successes, Morgan earned leadership of the Brotherhood of the Coast. Now numbering thousands, the buccaneers before long nearly paralyzed Spanish commerce.

In 1688, Morgan made two spectacular raids—one on Cuba, where he seized the city of Puerto Príncipe, and another on Panama, where he captured the city of Portobello with a force of 500 men. He overcame the castle's defenders, looted the town, and forced the payment of a large ransom in gold and silver coins. After sailing back to Port Royal in Jamaica, his men quickly squandered the loot in debauchery.

Trying to get even, the Spanish made some weak raids in Jamaica. To outdo them, Morgan decided to seize Panama City, Spain's principal treasure port for the transfer of gold and silver brought up by ship from South America. (Remember Drake's conquest of Panama in 1572?) Panama now had a population of about 6,000. Late in 1670, Morgan assembled 38 ships and 2,000 men and, with the biggest fleet ever seen in the Caribbean, sailed again for Panama.

He captured defense works on the coast, shifted to canoes to go up the Chagres River, and then made a grueling march through the jungle to reach the city of Panama. The buccaneers encountered about 1,200 Spanish troops on foot and another 400 on horses. But they were raw recruits and no match for Morgan's tough veterans. In a pitched battle, the defense force lost some 500 killed or wounded, while Morgan lost only 15 men.

But much of Panama's treasure had been loaded onto ships while Morgan was marching through the jungle. As the defense force retreated, they exploded buildings, setting huge fires that burned down all but the stones of the cathedral. The enraged Morgan tortured the survivors cruelly in order to learn where any money was hidden. He managed to amass a pile of loot, and then with some 600 prisoners and a mule train loaded with silver and other valuables, he marched his men back through the jungle to their ships.

News of the destruction of Panama enraged the Spanish government, for Spain was now officially at peace with England. Spain demanded that Morgan be punished. England tried to worm out of responsibility by blaming the sack of Panama on a bunch of pirates. Well then, said Spain, bring Morgan, their leader, to justice.

So Morgan was arrested and shipped to England, presumably to await trial. But two years passed and he was never put in prison. Instead he was knighted by the King and sent back to Jamaica as deputy governor, charged with building up that island's defense. Taking his duties lightly, Morgan

enjoyed himself to the fullest, enlarging his estates, and drinking and gambling in the taverns of Port Royal. Neither bullet nor sword nor hangman's noose ended his days, but rather the ill effects of dissolute living. He lived to 1688, the honored Sir Henry Morgan.

Captain Subatol Deul

Some of the Jews driven out of Spain in 1492 by their Catholic Majesties, Ferdinand and Isabella, turned to piracy to survive. They took special joy in capturing Spanish ships carrying cargoes of gold and precious goods extracted from the Americas by the conquistadors. Beginning with Christopher Columbus, the conquistadors suffered no pangs of conscience as they plundered the New World and enslaved or exterminated the Native Americans.

There are only scanty reports of the deeds of Jewish pirates. But one man's name that has come down to us is Captain Subatol Deul. His ship marauded along the coasts of South America in the first half of the 1600s. Little is known of Deul's early life except that his father was said to be a great physician who traveled widely and mastered many languages. How his son became a pirate we do not know. He seems to have had a privateer's commission from the British to make war on their enemy, the Spanish. But like many other adventurers who found piracy profitable, he may not have bothered to get official approval for his sea raids.

Captain Deul joined other pirates who sailed on the Pacific side of the Americas. They rendezvoused at a small harbor on the coast of Chile. In 1640, that band of buccaneers suffered defeat when the Spanish navy mustered sufficient firepower against them. Some pirates were killed in the battle, but though Deul lost his ship, he managed to escape capture.

He found refuge among local Indians, who treated him kindly because he had never abused them. Although Deul would have liked to return to Europe, he was helpless without a ship. So he lived out his days among the Indians, marrying the daughter of a tribal chief.

OPPOSITE:
Captain Subatol Deul

One day—it is not certain when this happened—Deul was wandering about when he came across a smelting furnace, used to refine ore. It stood alone, with no one around. Testing the metal, he found it to be gold. But from where? Prowling through the area, he came across the mouth of a cave, almost hidden by boulders and piled-up brush. He made his way in and saw Indians cutting into the rock with primitive hand tools. He learned they had been supervised by a lone Spaniard who had fled when he heard a prowler outside. It appeared that the Spaniard was running the mining operation secretly, in order to avoid paying the tax on gold demanded by the Spanish colonial administration.

Deul took over the mine, and as the gold piled up, he buried it in an underground vault. It was said that the gold extracted from the mine amounted to some 6,000 pounds by the time Deul died. It never left the vault, because Deul had no means to carry it to Europe.

Long after, in 1926, a farmer named Manuel Castro, who had heard the story of hidden treasure, tried to find Deul's buried gold. He failed to locate it, but he did find an earthen jug with some documents in it. They were written and signed by Deul. The language was Spanish—but mixed with Hebrew characters. What the documents said, we do not know. Jews in Spain who, although baptized and showing some signs of Christianity, privately kept to the ceremony and ritual of Judaism were known as Marranos. So Marrano came to mean "secret Jew." It is known that some Marranos wrote using Spanish mixed with Hebrew characters. So the documents seemed to confirm the belief that Captain Subatol Deul came from a Marrano family

A Private Republic

By the late seventeenth century, buccaneers had grown so threatening that the major European powers in the Caribbean took strong measures to drive them out. Some of the buccaneers moved their base of operations to the island of Madagascar, where they established what was known as "The Private Republic of Libertaria."

Trading in Madagascar

Madagascar is the world's fourth largest island, situated about 800 miles below the equator, off the southeast coast of Africa. It stretches 980 miles north to south, and is about 260 miles across at its widest point. England is only one–fifth its size, and Italy half its size. Madagascar's people are not of African stock. It is believed they migrated to the island from Indonesia.

Madagascar's sheltered harbors and abundant meat and citrus fruit made it an important trading place for both Arab and Indian merchants. Around 1690, pirates driven from the Caribbean were finding refuge in the island's ports. A colonial governor of New York wrote London that "the vast riches of the Red Sea and Madagascar are such a lure to seamen that there's almost

CAPTAIN KIDD

New York City in the late 1600s was something of a pirate haven, too, though not on the same scale as Madagascar. Many of its merchants connived with royal officials to make deals with pirates. Captain William Kidd, a Scot, cuddled up with local society figures as well as with the royal governor. They outfitted a ship under Kidd's command. Its aim was to hijack pirate cargoes in Far Eastern seas and bring the loot to New York, where it would be sold for the benefit of Kidd and his backers.

Kidd sailed for the Indian Ocean, but instead of the risky business of attacking pirate ships, he turned to piracy himself. He captured five ships off the coast of India and then headed for Madagascar. His piracy infuriated the Grand Moghul, who retaliated by threatening the trade of the British East India Company. The result: Captain Kidd was hauled into court and tried for his crimes. His illustrious backers (who included King William of Britain) remained silent, and in 1701, Kidd was found guilty and hanged.

no withholding them from turning pirate."

At that time only the coastal fringes of Madagascar held small settlements; the interior was unexplored. The pirates raided ships in the Indian Ocean and then retreated with their loot to the island harbors. Merchants with no conscience about dealing in stolen goods would come to buy the plunder—silks, spices, ivory, jewels—at a discount. In turn, they sold the pirates basic necessities—food, medicines, tools, rope, weapons—at greatly inflated prices.

So the pirates were themselves at times the prey of "honest" businessmen. Other merchants who dropped in at Madagascar to refresh and repair their ships on their way back to England's North American colonies were in the legal, if inhumane, business of slave trading.

It's no wonder that Madagascar became a pirate haven. No one owned it. No European power claimed it. The small local tribes dominated only a few bits and pieces of the island.

Pirates tired of their eternal wanderings made the island their home. Settlements of a few dozen "retired" pirates, along with their women and children and slaves, sprang up here and there, presided over by pirate chiefs who dubbed themselves "king." Some pirate settlers traded for a living or became planters. And all of them exploited the nearby natives.

By the end of the 1600s, you could always find a dozen pirate ships anchored in the island harbors, on their way to or from plundering cruises. American merchants became the backers of pirates bound for the Indian Ocean, as well as brokers for the loot stolen from the ships of Asian merchants. The people in the American colonies did not mind such dealings. When Thomas Tew, a pirate captain from Newport, Rhode Island, returned home from Madagascar, he was received respectfully. Especially when it was found that his piracy had made him very rich. The folks at home clung to romantic visions of pirates as gallant rogues, rather than seeing them as the thieves and killers they really were. Besides, they felt, weren't those Arab and Asian merchants heathens?

Eventually a myth began to build that ex-pirates in Madagascar had created a sort of utopian community called the "Republic of Libertaria." There is no evidence that it was a utopia. But when the British government received mounting protests from victims of piracy, it acted to eradicate the pirate haven in Madagascar. Parliament passed laws that helped reduce piracy in those waters.

Pirate Queen

A pirates' paradise, they called it. As early as A.D. 400, Chinese and Japanese pirates were operating on the seas around China and Southeast Asia. So damaging was piracy to trade that China and Japan often combined their naval forces to suppress this common enemy.

Much later, in the sixteenth and seventeenth centuries, European pirates appeared in Asian seas. They followed the European powers who were advancing their military and commercial strength in the Far East. English, Dutch, and Portuguese pirates entered these waters to prey upon both European and native shipping.

Chinese pirates created great dynasties that pillaged coastal waters and settlements from the seventeenth to the nineteenth century. One of their most successful chiefs was Ching Chi-ling, a Catholic convert whose power rivaled an emperor's. For more than 20 years, he commanded a fleet of 1,000 well-armed vessels and a private force of Dutch troops and ex-slaves. He ruled the coast between Guangzhou (Canton) and the Yangtze River until he was captured, imprisoned for 15 years, and executed in 1661. His son Koxinga took over, but when he died two years later, the pirate

Ching Shih

dynasty disintegrated into small groups.

The Chinese pirates used captured junks—traditional, flat-bottomed cargo vessels. The biggest, 100 feet long and 20 feet wide, were three-masted and weighed 600 tons. They could carry 400 men and 30 cannon. Their sails were made of bamboo matting held together with bamboo rods. Powerful oars helped them maneuver in tight corners or light winds. The captain and his family lived at the stern, while the crew slept on the open deck or in the hold.

Chinese pirates were not gentle with captives. Like any other pirates, they abused, tortured, and murdered prisoners. Their personal weapons were muskets, pistols, swords, knives, spears, blowpipes, and axes.

Chinese women, too, captained pirate ships. The most noted was Ching Shih, the widow of the pirate Ching Yih, who built up a great fleet that defied not only China's Imperial Navy but British warships as well. After he died in a storm, his wife proved herself to be a powerful, businesslike commander. She kept careful records of her illegal operations and pretended to respectability by calling her looting "the transshipment of goods."

At her peak she led a fleet of 800 large junks and about 1,000 smaller boats. Her crews included some 80,000 men and women. She could be as brutal as the worst of men. When her fleet raided and plundered coastal towns, she often burned them to the ground and kidnapped the inhabitants for ransom—or simply massacred them. She gave pirates rewards for returning from raids with the severed heads of victims slung around their necks.

Ching Shih's regime ended when quarrels among her pirates led to bloody clashes and the breakup of the fleet. In 1810, at Canton, she surrendered herself and the remnant of the fleet still under her control. She then disappeared from public view. It was rumored that she shifted her business talents to the less dangerous trade of smuggling.

But was Ching Shih the only woman to join the ranks of the pirates?

They Dressed Like Men

Ching Shih was not the only woman who dressed as a man and stalked the seas for loot. A century later another woman pirate in China won great notoriety. It happened in the 1920s, when China, beset by civil war, was unable to muster a strong defense against piracy. Many Western cargo ships were victimized by pirate crews under the command of Loi Chai-san, called "Queen of the Macao Pirates."

Macao is a small peninsula on a river estuary about 40 miles west of Hong Kong. Smugglers and pirates made it their base of operations, and Loi Choi-san, a small, harmless-appearing woman, acquired great wealth by relentless sea raids and through ransoming her captives. How and why she disappeared from history no one knows.

One of the earliest female pirate captains about whom legends sprang up is Alwinda. She enters Scandinavian history in the fifth century A.D., before the Viking era, as the daughter of a Swedish king. Confronted with an arranged marriage to Alf, the Prince of Denmark, she refused his hand and, with a group of female friends dressed as men, commandeered a ship and sailed off into the Baltic. At sea, they encountered a pirate crew that had just lost its captain. Not at all scared by fierce pirates, Alwinda behaved so imperiously that the men elected her their leader. Soon they were terrorizing shipping on the Baltic so badly that Prince Alf's father, the King of Denmark, determined to get rid of them. He sent his son out to track them down. His ship clashed with Alwinda's in a bloody battle that cost the lives of almost all the pirates but their captain. Alwinda surrendered, and when she removed her helmet, Alf recognized the woman he had desired to wed. And now, imbued with a new respect for Alf's fighting qualities, Alwinda changed her mind, agreed to marry him, and left the sea forever. Eventually she became the Queen of Denmark.

Much later, in the sixteenth century, the Irish pirate Grace O'Malley (known as "Grace of the Cropped Hair") preyed on shipping routes for 25 years. She was the daughter of a famous Irish family of sea rovers, who used their ships for fishing, trading, and piracy.

Born around 1530 in Connaught in the west of Ireland, at age sixteen Grace married a local chieftain, had three children, and soon lost her husband, probably through a clan fight. Grace then took command of the O'Malley fleet of some 20 ships. She married again, to another local chieftain. Grace and her sailors attacked and plundered merchant ships off the Irish coast so often that the merchants of Galway pressed the English governor of the province to send an expedition against her. She forced the expedition to retreat. In 1577, while raiding lands of an English lord, she was captured and jailed for 18 months. The lord justice denounced her as "a woman that hath been a great spoiler, and chief commander and director of thieves and murderers at sea to spoil this province."

Upon her husband's death in 1583, the widow Grace, under Irish custom, lost the right to her husband's lands. Refusing to accept financial hardship, she plundered other people's lands. The governor called her a rebel and a traitor and ordered a powerful force to Clare Bay, where it took possession of the O'Malley fleet.

Grace appealed by letter to Queen Elizabeth and then made a personal visit to the Queen. She claimed she had been forced to fight on land and sea to defend her property from aggressive neighbors. Elizabeth responded by ordering the governor to grant Grace "some maintenance for the rest of her living of her old age."

Now nearly seventy, Grace placed command of the O'Malley fleet in her sons' hands. She died around 1603.

Of Charlotte de Berry, a seventeenth-century pirate, not much is known beyond a few bare facts. She was born in England in 1636, and early on she determined she would go to sea. She married a sailor and, dressed as a man, followed him into the navy. One day her ship was seized by pirates bound for Africa. When the pirate captain attacked her, having discovered she was a woman, she fought back and cut off his head with her sword. The pirate crew was glad to get rid of a vicious captain and made this tough young woman their leader. Under her command they cruised the coast of Africa, capturing ships laden with cargoes of gold. How her life ended is unknown.

There may well have been more women who sailed the seas under pirate flags. But since those who did this had to dress like men, fight, drink, swear, and carouse like men, some no doubt escaped being unmasked as female, even in quarters as cramped as those on an eighteenth-century ship. In the case of women soldiers posing as men, there is solid evidence that some fought through wars without ever being found out. In modern times, several women have sailed around the world solo, proving their courage and their hardiness.

About 300 years ago, two women wrote vivid pages in the records of piracy. They were Mary Read and Anne Bonny, who for a time served on the same pirate ship and fought side by side.

Mary Read was born out of wedlock in Plymouth, England, around 1693. Her mother brought her up as a boy. At thirteen, Mary worked as a male servant. But seeking adventure, she quit and, dressed as a man, went to join the Royal Navy. Maintaining the disguise—a man's jacket, long trousers, and a scarf tied around her head—she soon switched to the army, and fought bravely in Flanders. In spite of her good record, she was not promoted, for in those days commissions were mostly bought and sold. Discouraged, Mary switched to a regiment of marines. There, she fell in love with a handsome officer and revealed herself to be a woman. The delighted young man promptly married her.

When discharged from the service, the couple set up a tavern and did well. But Mary's husband died soon after, and the business went downhill. Once again she put on men's clothing and rejoined the army. Ever restless, she deserted within a few months and found a berth on a Dutch merchant ship in the West Indies trade. She did so well as a sailor that the crew never realized she was a woman.

On her very first voyage, the ship was captured by English pirates. Thinking her the only Englishman aboard, they pressed her into their crew. Mary would always declare she became a pirate only under compulsion, intending to quit when the chance came. Maybe. But the records show she played as hardy and daring a role in the capture of ships of all nations as her fellow pirates did. None of them suspected her true sex.

In 1717, when the English Crown declared a general amnesty for pirates who would quit the illegal life, Mary left the sea and went to live on an island in the West Indies. When she ran out of money, she signed onto a privateering expedition. It was aboard this ship that Mary Read met Anne Bonny.

Anne had been born in Ireland. Her father, William Cormac, was a prominent lawyer who had the child by his maid, Peg Brennan. To conceal the truth from his wife, he dressed the child in male clothing and pretended she was a relative's boy he would raise to be his clerk. But his wife was not fooled, and to escape her fury, he sailed with the maid and the child for South Carolina, where he prospered as both a lawyer and merchant.

Although Anne, a red-haired beauty, was considered to be a fine catch for some wealthy man, she ignored her father's wishes and at sixteen married James Bonny, a poor young sailor. Infuriated, her father disowned her. Whereupon the young couple left for Nassau on New Providence island in the Caribbean, a hangout for pirates. Here, Anne met the pirate captain "Calico Jack" Rackham, so nicknamed because of his taste for flashy clothing made of calico material. She fell in love with the pirate, deserted her husband, and went off to sea with Rackham. He was a small-scale pirate who raided fishing boats and local merchant ships. When their ship met resistance, Anne fought as well as any sailor in the crew. One day they took the ship Mary

OPPOSITE:
Mary Read and
Anne Bonny

THEY DRESSED LIKE MEN   **59**

was sailing on, and still dressed as a man, Mary joined Rackham's crew.

Anne Bonny soon recognized that the newcomer was a woman, and the two, becoming fast friends, let Rackham in on the secret. On one of their pirate cruises a merchant ship was overtaken and a furious fight began in which almost every sailor aboard the merchantman was killed. Among the few who surrendered was a young navigator. Mary fell madly in love with him and soon told him she was a woman. A passionate love affair began.

One day Mary's lover quarreled so fiercely with another crew member that they decided to fight a duel when next they reached land. Soon their ship anchored off an island, and the duel was set for the next day. Mary, fearing her lover might be killed, picked a quarrel with the same pirate and got him to agree to meet her in a duel early the next morning, two hours before the time he was supposed to fight her lover. Slipping away before dawn, she met her opponent on the beach and, fighting better than any man he had ever encountered, killed him with her cutlass.

Rackham's piracy came to an end in 1720 when his ship was caught off the island of Jamaica by a fast sloop of the Royal Navy. A bloody battle began; when it was plain the pirates were losing, most of them, including Calico Jack, scuttled belowdecks. Only two stayed on top—Mary and Anne. Madly firing pistols and slashing savagely with their cutlasses, they fought on. When they saw they could not hold out any longer, Mary ran to the hatch and screamed down to the pirates below to "come up and fight like men!" But the crew only shrank back, and the enraged Mary fired both her pistols into them, killing one and wounding several others. It was too late to turn the tide; the battle was over.

The captives were taken to Port Royal, Jamaica, given a quick trial, and all, Mary and Anne included, were sentenced to be hanged. When the judge asked if anyone had anything to say that might mitigate the sentence, Anne and Mary replied, "Milord, we plead our bellies." It was the truth. Both women were pregnant. The court put off their execution until the birth of the babies, as the law specified in such cases.

On the day Captain Jack was to hang, Anne was allowed a last brief visit with him. Her only words were, "I'm sorry to see you there, Jack, but if you had fought like a man, you need not have been hanged like a dog."

Mary Read cheated the gallows, ironically, by falling prey to a fever in prison and dying before her child could be born. Anne was luckier. Some influential planters, who had done business with her father in Carolina, managed to get the Jamaican authorities to release her. Then she disappeared.

On the Barbary Coast

Piracy in the Mediterranean was as old as shipping itself. Much earlier, in Caesar's time, it had so infected the sea that it took a massive effort by the Roman navy to bring it to an end—temporarily.

Around A.D. 700, with the Muslim conquest of the Middle East, part of Spain, and all of North Africa, the Barbary states on the North African coast fell under Islamic control. They became semiautonomous provinces of the Turkish Empire.

As the conflict between Islam and the Christian states threatened to go on endlessly, ships of the Barbary states attacked the shipping trade of the Christian enemy. For centuries, the rulers of the North African states—Tunisia, Tripoli, Algeria, and Morocco—made large-scale piracy their main source of revenue. This wasn't piracy, they claimed, but privateering, an old and honorable way to wage war.

Christian sea raiders used the same excuse as they attacked the sea trade of the Islamic states. Both sides issued licenses to privateers. The Mediterranean was consumed by cruel, everyday war of this kind. Under such conditions, the line between piracy and privateering became almost impossible to draw.

Muslim piracy found a special set of victims in the late eleventh century, when the Christian powers launched the Crusades to drive Islam out of the Holy Land. The ships carrying the Crusaders to the Middle East often had

JEFFERSON AND THE PIRATES

After the American Revolution, Thomas Jefferson was sent to Paris as a diplomat and given the authority to make treaties with the Barbary pirates. He knew that to get their agreement would cost large sums. He would have preferred to win settlement with them by armed force. But the young American navy was too small and widely scattered to make threats believable.

So the new American republic did what the Europeans were doing: paid tribute to the pirates to protect the nation's shipping. Later, in 1801, when Jefferson became president, he sent warships to the Mediterranean to scare off the pirates. That led to war with the local ruler of Tripoli. Negotiations to end it failed until 1805, when settlement was reached.

U.S. prisoners were ransomed, and Tripoli renounced all rights to halt or levy tribute on American ships. It was the best bargain struck thus far with any Barbary state. But it did not end the threat of piracy to U.S. shipping. Not until 1815 did the U.S. stop paying tribute to any Barbary state. By 1830, European powers had taken control of the North African states and piracy on the Barbary coast came to an end.

wealthy nobles and knights aboard, great prizes for any pirate.

Christian missionaries were sent out to negotiate ransoms for the captive Crusaders. The rich could redeem themselves, but great numbers of the poor—seamen and soldiers—could not. They were sold into slavery. Tunis alone was said to hold more than 10,000 Christian slaves. Some nations trading in the Mediterranean thought it cheaper to pay blackmail to the pirates than to undertake an expensive war against them.

England, a maritime power that played a great role in the Crusades, had been indifferent to the inhumanity of slavery so long as blacks were the victims. But now that whites, and English whites at that, were being enslaved, the Crown took some action. Henry Mainwaring, a pirate recently pardoned for his sins, was put in command of a squadron of ships and sent to the Barbary coast to drive the pirates out. He failed in his mission.

Flourishing Muslim piracy also induced many English and Dutch pirates to try their luck in the Mediterranean. They plundered the ships of Genoa, Malta, and their own countries until the Muslims got tired of the competition and tracked down and enslaved some of the intruders. Piracy of this nature was really a secondary form of war. These upstart sea captains replaced tired kings and emperors, and international conflicts degenerated into a free-for-all in the Mediterranean.

European pirates had no aim other than to get rich. So many "turned

Turk," as they put it, and entered the service of Muslim pirate chiefs. Christians went over to the Turks and Islam by the thousands. There was no rigid barrier between the two enemy religions. People passed to and fro, indifferent to states or creeds. For profit, they seized the opportunity for conspiracy or betrayal provided by circumstances.

Sir Francis Verney is an example of an Englishman who turned Turk. The Muslim pirates welcomed him because of his superior technical skills and his knowledge of European shipping. He paid a portion of his profits from plunder to one of the Barbary chiefs. But after raiding a number of English ships, he was taken prisoner by a Sicilian galley, enslaved, and chained to an oar. Broken in body and spirit, he died within two years, at the age of thirty-one. Life for a galley slave was brutal and short. Hunger, beatings, and mutilation soon ended the horror of that existence.

Why would an aristocrat like Verney become a highwayman or pirate? Money is the answer. The aristocracy during that time (and later, too!) was often in financial trouble. Some had been ruined by one means or another, others were the younger sons of families of small fortunes. They knew, too, that thieves on land or sea were often backed by powerful forces.

Well into the nineteenth century, the Barbary pirates were the terror of mariners. When they squeezed past the Straits of Gibraltar, they raided up and down the west coast of Europe, even as far as Northern Ireland, and threatened shipping across the Atlantic.

Some of the Muslim pirates achieved great power. Turgut Reis, once a slave on a Christian galley for five years, was a most terrifying pirate. A commander of great skill and daring, he led a fleet of pirate ships to Tripoli in 1551 and captured it from the Christian Knights of Malta.

Then there were the brothers Barbarossa. Not Turks, but men of Greek origin converted to Islam, their red hair earned them the name of Barbarossa, or Redbeard. One of them, Aruj, managed to capture Algiers in 1516. After his death in 1518, his brother Khayr ad-Din was made governor-general of Algiers by the Turkish emperor, Sultan Selim I, and given a force of 2,000 sol-

diers. Commanding the sultan's fleets, he raided the Christian towns of the Mediterranean and captured dozens of merchant ships. He died in 1546, after bringing Muslim power in the Mediterranean to its peak.

The great threat to sea traffic posed by both Muslim and Christian pirates had an interesting consequence. In the sixteenth century, land traffic began to expand at the expense of sea traffic. Land routes had long been a miserable way to travel, or to transport goods, because of the terrible condition of the roads almost everywhere. Now old roads were improved and new roads built to accommodate heavier traffic.

Both a cause and a consequence of the growing importance of land routes was the greater use of mules. They proved to be more powerful and hard-working than horses or other animals. In the New World, endless processions

of mules hauled gold and silver, piled up by Spanish conquest to and from ports. This, in turn, led pirates on the Spanish main to make the mule trains a special target.

People: The Richest Prize

Slavery is often linked with piracy in the records of that robber trade. In ancient Greece, the threat of enslavement by pirates was so widespread that people moved their settlements away from the coast. Families traveling by ship were often captured by pirates and sold into slavery. The agony of a family's separation was used by classical dramatists, who wrote scenes of re-union between parents and their children, whom pirates had snatched away long ago.

But seagoing thugs operating for their own profit were not the only ones who menaced people's security. Respectable Greek city-states hired pirate ships to attack foreign vessels and seize their valuable goods. The best prize was always a catch of human beings. These sad souls, if rich enough, were held for ransom, while the others were sold on the auction block.

The Illyrian pirates in the Adriatic often hired themselves out to the neighboring kings of Macedon. The kings used them in wars against rival powers and to loot merchant ships and enslave the crews and passengers. Then there were the pirates of Cilicia (located on the southern coast of Asia Minor), whose fleet served Mithridates VI, a king of Asia Minor. Their specialty was slave-running. They raided coastal towns so ruthlessly that whole areas saw their populations disappear into slavery. Rome, as we've seen, finally had to take drastic measures to halt the plague of piracy.

But the pirates did not give up entirely. In the Red Sea and the Black Sea, there were occasional outbursts of piracy because the Roman fleets neglected those waters. The Roman world had to rely more on the peacetime methods of enslavement: slavery by birth, sales from border tribes, penal sentence to servitude.

So long as the desire for slave labor persisted, there were always men eager to profit from it. Piracy was considered a good business to meet a scarcity or satisfy a growing demand. The traffic in slaves became one of the earliest forms of commerce. Men, women, and children seized by pirates on land or sea were sent as commodities to wherever their muscle, skill, beauty, or brains would bring the highest price.

Pirates had no scruples about enslaving their own people. The Danish pirates paid a tax to their king for the privilege of looting the "barbarians" living around the Norwegian Sea. But often they abused the privilege to turn treacherously upon their own countrymen. A chronicle of this period says that "As soon as one has caught his neighbor, he sells him ruthlessly as a slave, to either friend or stranger."

In the fifteenth century, both naval vessels and merchant ships used forced labor to row their galleys. Men convicted of crimes were often sentenced to the galleys. When there were not enough convicts on hand to fill the oars, navies bought men captured by pirates. It was one reason why Europeans backed Christian pirates to track down Muslim ships, manning their galleys through such slave raids. The Christian Knights of Malta, pirates themselves, considered the use of Muslim galley slaves to be a religious obligation. It's hard to decide whether the short and cruel life of a galley slave was better than the quick death that came when the Maltese slaughtered captive Muslims unfit for pulling the oars.

In the seventeenth century, as the French and Spanish enlarged their naval fleets, more and more galley slaves were in demand. While criminals and religious minorities were put to the oars, governments sent out agents to buy up strong males captured by pirates on the Barbary coast or the Eastern shores of the Mediterranean. It didn't matter whether a fresh lot of slaves came from the crews or the passengers, or what their origin was. Chained to the oars were not only Muslims, but Russian, Greek, and Jewish captives.

When the Jews were expelled from Spain in 1492, and from Portugal the next year, they took ships for foreign lands, where they hoped to start new lives. Many of those ships were seized by Mediterranean pirates, who took whatever of value the captives had. Those who appeared to have no money, the pirates often slaughtered, ripping their bellies open with swords to find the golden coins they might have swallowed. The younger males were chained to the oars or sold into slavery

It was around this time, the late fifteenth century, that the Portuguese became the first Europeans to establish trading posts on the west coast of Africa. They brought in European manufactured goods and exchanged them for African gold, ivory, and spices. Other Europeans soon competed for this lucrative trade. The English, French, Swedish, and Dutch all built trading forts along the African coast.

Now the prime commodity bought and sold became human beings. For plantation colonies established in North America and the Caribbean were looking for the cheapest labor to cultivate crops such as sugarcane and cotton. And soon Africans captured and enslaved by black kings and chieftains and then sold to white traders for transport across the Atlantic to America became the most profitable "product." Better to deal in than gold or ivory. Slaves could be sold in the Americas for 15 to 20 times their cost in Africa. Many, however, never reached port. They died during the "Middle Passage," crossing the Atlantic. Forced as they were into holds, with no sanitation, disease could spread rapidly. Sometimes Africans aboard slave ships revolted, though there was little chance to escape. The rebels were savagely repressed, whipped, shot, tossed overboard.

In the sixteenth century, the English entered the slave trade through Sir John Hawkins. Hearing "that Negroes were very good merchandise," in 1562 he led three ships from Plymouth to the African coast of Guinea, where he collected 300 blacks, "partly by the sword and partly by other means," as he put it. Which meant by kidnapping and piracy: raiding African villages and looting Portuguese ships. Then Hawkins sailed across the Atlantic to Hispaniola, where he sold the slaves for hides, ginger, sugar, and pearls. Back in Europe, he sold these goods for a handsome profit. So handsome that Queen Elizabeth invested in his next slaving expedition.

Sniffing high profits in that corner of the world, pirates began to operate

FOLLOWING PAGES:
Slavery

off the African coast. As always, they preyed on any kind of merchant ship, but hunted especially for slavers. When they captured a slave ship, they demanded a large ransom to let the voyage continue. The owners or captains readily paid, knowing their human cargo would bring a huge profit when sold on the other side of the Atlantic.

Pirates showed no more sympathy for the black captives belowdecks than the slavers had felt. Most pirates did not enter the transatlantic slave trade themselves; they preferred to sell the captive ships back to their owners. Some pirates, however, set up their own secret trading settlements in African river deltas and bought people directly from the African dealers.

That triangle of trade brought such immense profits that in 1672 Charles II chartered the Royal African Company, giving it a monopoly on the slave trade and all other commerce on the Guinea coast. England became the world's greatest slave trader. Not until 1833 did England abolish the slave trade throughout her empire. In the United States, it took the North's victory in the long and bloody Civil War to end slavery.

Runaway slaves often found a haven aboard a pirate ship. Such fugitives might make up as much as a third of the crew. A pirate's life with all its risks, including hanging, promised to be better than the dreadful conditions of slavery. Pirate captains, of course, were not out to rescue slaves or abolish slavery. And as we have seen, they sometimes took a direct hand in enslavement, raiding coastal plantations to capture slaves they would sell elsewhere.

In the West Indies, where piracy was common, slaves on the plantations heard stories of the welcome pirates gave to fugitives. In Martinique, for example, 50 blacks rose up against their French master and fled the island, hoping to find berths on pirate ships.

Once aboard a pirate ship, blacks were rarely treated as equals, though there are reports of a few who became ship's officers. Pirates were like most white people in the Western world, then and now, prejudiced believers in white superiority. They viewed people of color as inferiors or even as less than human. Some pirates sold blacks as commodities and used them as servants or slaves aboard ships. They were made to do the hard and dirty work: man the pumps, lug the food and water from shore to ship, wash the clothes, scrub the decks.

Pirates could show supreme indifference to the fate of slaves. In January 1722, the pirate captain Bartholomew Roberts entered the port of Whydah, a center for the slave trade on the west coast of Africa. About a dozen ships were at anchor. All but one surrendered to the pirates, agreeing to pay Roberts ransom for their vessels. When the commander of the English slave ship the *Porcupine* refused to pay ransom, Roberts's men tarred the deck of the ship so that it would burn easily, and then set it afire. The 80 slaves on board were chained together in pairs. A contemporary account said that the Africans were "under miserable choice of perishing by fire or water: those who jumped over board were seized by sharks, a voracious fish in plenty...and in their sight torn limb from limb alive."

In the World Today

Piracy has never died out. In some parts of the world it is still common: Southeast Asia, West Africa, the Caribbean. Offshore waters here are still danger zones. As long as merchant ships continue to carry valuable cargo across the world's seas, there will be pirates eager to attack and loot them.

The smaller the merchant ship, the greater the chance it will be attacked. Modern cargo boats that are huge are protected from assault at sea. But the smaller ones, carrying such goods as computers, watches, TV sets, are vulnerable to sudden sallies out of hidden coves by fast power launches.

Pleasure yachts sailing the Caribbean are a prime target, too. The ships themselves cost a fortune, that fact alone making them a worthwhile risk, and the rich passengers aboard make easy pickings. Even the gigantic cargo boats, when at anchor in port, may suffer piratical raids, because the small crew on duty can be forced to give over whatever can be carried off.

Modern piracy   In the Far East, pirates operate frequently against merchant shipping. In the 1990s, at least 90 attacks a year between Singapore and Sumatra were reported. The merchant ships are often small and manned by small crews. It takes only a handful of heavily armed pirates to terrify a crew and rob a vessel of whatever it carries. In these waters pirates often use fishing boats to which powerful engines have been added, or high–speed motorboats. A single successful raid can reap millions in profit when the cargo is sold.

Pirates of today are no gentler with their victims than in the past. Armed robbery, whether on land or on sea, often ends in devastating injuries or death.

Yet piracy now has less chance to succeed than in the old days, thanks to modern technology. The world's navies patrol waters important to their shipping, and radio and radar equipment connect ship to ship and ship to shore. Military and police aircraft fly over endangered waters to warn of possible trouble.

Still, modern piracy has chalked up successes, often at hideous cost to the victims. Everyone has read of refugees fleeing from their native land in open boats, desperate to escape brutal oppression or poverty, only to be attacked by pirates who rob them of their pitiful belongings.

Another form of modern piracy does not inflict personal violence but nevertheless robs its victims of their legal property. This form of piracy usually entails violation of international copyright laws. These international laws were adopted to protect creators from theft of what they have produced. For every copy of a book sold, for instance, the author must be paid a royalty—a certain percentage of the sale price. This would be true, too, of a film, a piece of music, a TV program, a video. Thieves might copy a movie or TV program off a cable network, for example, and then sell prints at a discount to customers willing to buy stolen goods. Perhaps the customers do not even know the goods are pirated.

Or take radio. The Federal Communications Commission (FCC) requires that you obtain a license to establish a radio broadcasting station with an allotted wavelength or frequency. But in 1996, for instance, a radio transmitter and makeshift studio were set up in a New York apartment and "Steal This Radio" began weekly pirate broadcasts, transmitting live and recorded music. So common did this practice become that an enterprising publisher printed a *Complete Manual of Pirate Radio* to show anyone with minimum knowledge how to set up a pirate radio station very clearly.

That same year, 36 people were arrested for producing and distributing millions of videotapes of first-run American films and Asian karate and pornographic films. A sophisticated nationwide operation produced about 100,000 pirated videos a week, grossing $500,000 a week. The thieves made their own blank tapes, copied stolen videos in round–the–clock factories, distributed the pirated tapes, and even franchised their operation for a fee. The videos were slickly packaged and even brazenly carried the standard FBI warnings about such illegal reproduction.

In Communist China, copyright piracy occurs on a vast scale. All over the country, counterfeit compact discs, videos, and computer software sell for a pittance. Whether it's a video of *Apollo 13* or a CD of arias sung by Luciano Pavarotti, shoppers find a wide range of music, movies, and software, all sold in violation of international copyright laws.

Despite an agreement China made with the U.S. government to stop it, the piracy of intellectual property continues. In 1995 alone, 220 million cassette tapes, and 45 million CDs, a total of $250 million, were copied illegally. In Guangdong, a province on the southeast coast of China, 19 factories were violating copyright laws at some time or another. China has been "the largest producer of pirated music in the world," said *The New York Times*, and "one of the five largest of pirated software."

For a while in 1996, the Chinese closed 15 factories doing this illegal work, prosecuted scores of individuals, and shut down distribution centers and theaters showing stolen movies. They also agreed to stop selling pirated materials abroad. But it has been reported that nearby on the Portuguese island of Macao, illegal factories now smuggle in roughly 500,000 pirated compact discs every day. Everyone likes to get things cheap, but at the expense of the creators?

Mexico City is home to one of the world's biggest bazaars for illegal copies of videos, music cassettes, and software. One day, a Walt Disney movie not even out on video in the United States was on sale there. Hundreds of vendors hawk their wares in open-air stalls, just blocks from police headquarters. Mexico has laws protecting intellectual property but grossly fails to enforce them. A government agency listed the losses for 1995 from the piracy of U.S. products in Mexico: records and music, $85 million; books, $33 million; movies, $67 million; computer entertainment software, $100 million.

The five countries where the most piracy occurred in 1995 were given as China, $1,835 million; Russia, $726 million; Italy, $515 million; Mexico, $285 million; Brazil, $273 million.

Buried Treasure

Robert Louis Stevenson's *Treasure Island*, that evergreen tale of pirates' loot buried on a Caribbean island, has charmed readers young and old for more than a hundred years. Many other pirate stories also feature treasure hidden by sea robbers. The belief in buried booty is so widely held that hunters have roamed the world looking for these secret caches of gold.

But very rarely has such buried treasure been found. Yes, some lucky divers have recovered treasure from sunken ships, but these were Spanish treasure ships, not the ships of pirates. Spain lost many vessels carrying treasure extracted from the mines of her colonies. They sank in storms at sea or, as the victims of pirate attacks, went down under cannonading before pirates could board them. Such a one was the Spanish galleon that sank in the West Indies, located in 1686 by Sir William Phips. He brought to the surface more than a million dollars' worth of gold and silver.

Business enterprises have been formed to search for treasures lost at sea, especially off the Florida coast. People have invested millions of dollars in ships, divers, and special equipment in the hope of finding fortune. The famous *Mary Rose*, belonging to King Henry VIII, sank in 1545. In 1967, after 12 years of search and 28 separate diving expeditions, the ship was found. But only a third of the hull was intact, and in it there was no treasure.

Better luck blessed treasure seekers when they found the *Whydah*, a ship that sank in 1717 when it struck a sandbar off Wellfleet, on Cape Cod. The huge *Whydah*, formerly engaged in the slave trade, was three-masted, weighed 300 tons, and was 100 feet long. In May, 1717, Sam Bellamy, a pirate captain, was cruising in the Caribbean when he encountered the slave ship heading back to England after a voyage that had taken her from London to Africa for slaves and ivory and then across the Atlantic to Jamaica. Selling the slaves to planters, the *Whydah* had picked up fresh cargo for the return voyage. The *Whydah* did not resist the pirates, and when Bellamy boarded the ship he found great riches: ivory, indigo, sugar, and much gold and silver. Bellamy converted the *Whydah* into a 28-gun pirate ship and headed north up the Atlantic coast.

Diving for buried treasure

When the *Whydah* sank during heavy fog, Captain Bellamy and most of the 146 pirates aboard were drowned. The nine seamen who reached shore were tried for piracy in Boston, and seven were hanged. A search for the ship began in 1982, and in 1984 the wreck was found. It is perhaps the only pirate ship to have been positively identified. On it was a ship's bell with *Whydah* clearly marked. Excavations brought up a great quantity of Spanish gold coins, gold bars, gold nuggets, bits of gold, and gold dust, as well as thousands of Spanish silver coins. Nearly 400 pieces of African jewelry were scattered in the wreck, mostly gold beads, pendants, and ornaments.

Besides the ship's guns, 15 grenades were found. These were an early form of hand grenade which, when tossed onto the deck of a ship, would explode with deadly force. The many other artifacts in the wreck included 28 lead

gaming pieces, an indication of how popular gambling was among the pirates.

Such finds are of great interest to archaeologists trying to reconstruct the life of the past. Treasure hunters, however, are not seeking artifacts. The odds are strongly against them, for not many pirates found great wealth when they looted the holds of merchant ships. And what they did find of value was divided up among them according to rank, and in most cases quickly spent ashore, on liquor, gambling, and debauchery.

The pirates themselves were beguiled by fantastic tales of other pirates who had made their fortune. Most pirates, if lucky, might enjoy only briefly a sum of money a bit beyond what an honest seaman could earn in a lifetime. Few ever piled up a fortune.

No, buried pirate treasure is far more common in literature than in life. In

1843, exactly forty years before *Treasure Island* appeared, Edgar Allan Poe in his short story "The Gold Bug" gave credence to buried pirate treasure, this time on an island off South Carolina. Poe used legends about Captain Kidd to create the fictional discovery of a buried chest containing $1.5 million in gold and jewels.

Figures of Romance

"Pirates were no more than common criminals," writes David Cordingly, formerly of Britain's National Maritime Museum, "but we still see them as figures of romance…The picture which most of us have turns out to be a blend of historical facts with three centuries of ballads, melodramas, epic poems, romantic novels, adventure stories, comic strips, and films. In the process pirates have acquired a romantic aura…which they certainly never deserved."

The best-known and most influential of all books on pirates is *Treasure Island*. What reader could resist the lure: "Dreadful stories they were: about hanging, and walking the plank, and storms at sea, and the Dry Tortugas, and wild deeds and places on the Spanish Main," wrote Stevenson.

Stevenson's novel, meant for boys but loved as much by adults, created the enduring character of Long John Silver. Although he was neither a seaman nor a pirate, Stevenson's thorough research and his imagination give the book its power. It's no wonder that when we hear the word *pirate*, we think not of a murderous thief but of that charming rascal, a one-legged man stumping about the deck with a parrot on his shoulder.

Long John Silver was preceded thousands of years earlier by other literary pirates. In Homer's *Odyssey*, the Cyclops asks of Odysseus and his men, "Strangers, who are you? Are you here for trade? Or have you wandered recklessly over the sea like pirates who go about risking their necks to bring trouble on others?" And as we've seen, Odysseus proved to be one of those piratical wanderers.

Pirates figure in Miguel de Cervantes's classic novel, *Don Quixote*. The Span-

No one had a greater influence on pirate literature than the English journalist and novelist Daniel Defoe (1660?-1731). The son of a London candlemaker, in his early twenties Defoe began a career as a pamphleteer, using his pen to advocate such liberal measures as the income tax, insurance, road improvement, and insane asylum. A dogged dissenter and fighter for religious liberty, he outraged both of Britain's dominant political parties and was briefly imprisoned.

At sixty, still wonderfully energetic, Defoe turned to fiction, writing Robinson Crusoe, which made him famous overnight. Then came three other novels—tales of adventurous rogues, male and female—which delighted a rising new middle class fed up with the pieties of the decaying feudal world.

When Defoe read Exquemelin's Buccaneers of America (1678), an immensely popular account of the gory deeds of pirates, he set about concocting his own mixture of fiction with fact to depict a large number of pirate captains. Writers who followed Defoe down into the twentieth century borrowed their pirate villains freely from him.

ish Cervantes himself was captured by Barbary pirates in 1515 and endured five years of slavery in Algiers. He was finally freed when his family raised the ransom. Cervantes also wrote plays in which pirates figure.

The Scottish writer Sir Walter Scott is best known for his novel *Ivanhoe*, but a lesser work of his is *The Pirate*. Another nineteenth-century novelist, the Englishman Charles Kingsley, featured Elizabethan privateers in his popular story *Westward Ho!* He endowed them with godliness, manliness, and patriotism, while ignoring their criminal acts of violence and robbery.

Numbers of children have seen J. M. Barrie's play *Peter Pan*. It tells the story of the defeat of pirates by a boy who never grows up. Peter's enemy is the more-than-life-size pirate Captain Hook, portrayed as both evil and laughable by a host of famous actors on stage and screen. Some 50 years after Barrie wrote his play, Walt Disney produced an animated film version of *Peter Pan*, but re-created it as a musical comedy. It had no link to reality and made the pirates harmless and amusing. Within a year, the Broadway stage presented *Peter Pan* as a musical comedy, again with no hint of the reality of piracy. The production has been shown on television several times since then.

In Gilbert and Sullivan's *Pirates of Penzance*, a comic opera, the pirates' victims ask for pity on the grounds that they are orphans. Their plea makes the softhearted pirates refuse to rob them, as they confess that they, too, are orphans. And in the end everyone turns out to be "noblemen who have gone wrong." Gilbert and Sullivan's pirates poke fun at historical reality, satirizing the romantic view.

In his twenties, the English poet Lord Byron wrote a verse narrative called *The Corsair*, which helped enlarge the romantic myth of piracy. Byron projected himself as the image of a heroic pirate, Conrad, excusing his crimes with the lines: "He knew himself a villain but he deem'd / The rest no better than the thing he seem'd."

An instant success, *The Corsair* sold 10,000 copies on its first day of publication. In turn, it inspired several operas (one by Verdi), a ballet, and an overture by Berlioz. In the classic children's adventure tales by Arthur Ransome, the author–illustrator, pirates play a big role. Two girls are pirates in *Swallows and Amazons*, and in *Peter Duck* children embark on a hunt for buried pirate treasure.

One of the most popular writers to weave piracy into fiction was Daphne du Maurier. Her 1941 best–seller was *Frenchman's Creek*, a romance set in the time of King Charles I of England. At its heart is the love of a highborn Englishwoman for a Frenchman who has taken to piracy out of boredom and to gain wealth. He robs merchant ships but gives alms to the poor. He avoids violence if at all possible, preferring to take prizes by superior seamanship and brilliant tactics. Soon after publication, the novel was made into a movie.

There have been almost too many movies about piracy to count. Jan Rogozinski, whose encyclopedia of piracy is superb, reports that dozens of films presenting the spectacular, swashbuckling fantasy of piracy were made from the days of the old silent films to the 1990s. They crackle with action— sword duels, sea battles, mutinies. Most are set in the Caribbean between 1680 and 1720. The most frequently filmed story has been *Treasure Island;* the pirates most often portrayed are Blackbeard, Captain Kidd, and Sir Henry Morgan. Later, the stock formula of the swashbuckler gave way to comic treatments, with pirate life parodied.

SELECTED BIBLIOGRAPHY

Brandsted, Johannes. *The Vikings*. Baltimore: Penguin, 1967.

Braudel, Fernand. *The Mediterranean and the Mediterranean World in the Age of Philip II*. 2 vols. New York: Harper & Row, 1972–73.

——*The Wheels of Commerce: Civilization and Capitalism 15th-18th Century*. New York: Harper & Row, 1972.

Burg, B. R. *Sodomy and the Pirate Tradition: English Sea Rovers in the 17th Century Caribbean*. New York: New York University Press, 1984.

Burlingame, Roger. *The American Conscience*. New York: Knopf, 1957.

Casson, Lionel. *The Ancient Mariners*. Princeton: Princeton University Press, 1991.

Cordingly, David. *Under the Black Flag*. New York: Random House, 1996.

Dow, George Francis, and John Henry Edmonds. *The Pirates of the New England Coast: 1630–1730*. New York: Argosy, 1968.

Esquemeling, John. *The Buccaneers of America*. Winston, ME: Corner House, 1976.

Finley, M. I. *Aspects of Antiquity*. New York: Viking, 1968.

Friedman, Ellen G. *Spanish Captives in North Africa in the Early Modern Age*. Madison: University of Wisconsin, 1983.

Gross, David. *The Jewish People's Almanac*. New York: Hippocrene, 1994.

Marsden, John. *The Fury of the Northmen*. New York: St. Martin's, 1995.

Meltzer, Milton. *Slavery: A World History*. New York: Da Capo, 1993.

Parry, J. H. *The Age of Reconnaissance*. Berkeley: University of California, 1981.

Platt, Cameron, and John Wright. *Treasure Islands: The Fascinating World of Pirates, Buried Treasure, and Fortune Hunters*. Golden, CO: Fulcrum, 1995.

Reynolds, Robert L. *Europe Emerges: 600–1750*. Madison: University of Wisconsin, 1961.

Rogozinski, Jan. *Pirates: An A–Z Encyclopedia*. New York: Da Capo, 1996.

Sawyer, P. H. *Kings and Vikings*. New York: Barnes & Noble, 1994.

Sherry, Frank. *Raiders and Rebels: The Golden Age of Piracy*. New York: Hearst Marine Books, 1986.

Snow, Edward R. *Pirates and Buccaneers of the Atlantic Coast*. Boston: Yankee Publishing, 1944.

Stanley, Jo., ed. *Bold in Her Breeches: Women Pirates Across the Ages*. New York: HarperCollins, 1995.

Sugden, John. *Sir Francis Drake*. New York: Holt, 1990.

Wolf, Eric R. *Europe and the People Without History*. Berkeley: University of California, 1982.

Youings, Joyce, ed. *Raleigh in Exeter: Privateering and Colonization in the Reign of Elizabeth I*. Exeter: University of Exeter, 1985.

ABOUT THE AUTHOR

Milton Meltzer has published more than 100 books for young readers and adults in the fields of history, biography, and social issues. He has also dealt with such diverse topics as the horse, gold, the potato, memory, and names. He has written and edited for newspapers, magazines, radio, television, and films.

Piracy and Plunder is his second book for Dutton. It was preceded by *Ten Queens: Portraits of Women of Power.*

Among the many honors for his books are five nominations for the National Book Award, as well as the Christopher, Jane Addams, Carter G. Woodson, Jefferson Cup, Washington Book Guild, Olive Branch, Golden Kite, and Regina awards. Many of his books have been chosen for the honor lists of the American Library Association, the National Council of Teachers of English, and the National Council for the Social Studies, as well as for the New York Public Library and *The New York Times* annual Best Books of the Year lists. He is also the recent recipient of the Laura Ingalls Wilder Award, which honors an author whose books have made, over a period of years, a substantial and lasting contribution to children's literature.

Meltzer and his wife, Hildy, live in New York City. They have two daughters, Jane and Amy, and two grandsons, Benjamin and Zachary. Mr. Meltzer is a member of the Authors Guild, American PEN, and the Organization of American Historians.

ABOUT THE ILLUSTRATOR

Bruce Waldman is a printmaker, painter, freelance illustrator, and designer whose work has been exhibited all over the world, including New York, Israel, Holland, Belgium, Japan, Colombia, and India. His etchings have been displayed in a contemporary print exhibition at the Metropolitan Museum of Art, as well as numerous permanent collections in the United States and abroad.

Mr. Waldman illustrated the cover for the best-selling *Iron John: A Book About Men,* by Robert Bly. He has also illustrated a number of limited signed editions of contemporary classics by authors such as T. Coraghessan Boyle, Martin Cruz Smith, E. L. Doctorow, and Chaim Potok, among others. He has been a member of the faculty of the School of Visual Arts in New York City for the past twenty years.

Mr. Waldman lives in Westfield, New Jersey, with his wife and two children.

INDEX

(Page numbers in *italics* refer to illustrations.)